Moku'ula

Maui's Sacred Island

Ua lehulehu a manomano ka ʻikena a ka Hawaiʻi
Great and numerous is the knowledge of the Hawaiians

ʻŌlelo Noʻeau 2814

This publication is sponsored by Bishop Museum's Native Hawaiian Culture and Arts Program in celebration of the Legacy of Excellence of Native Hawaiian culture. The Legacy of Excellence volumes are devoted to generating an appreciation of Native Hawaiian traditions, art, and language through education, awareness, and recognition of excellence in Native Hawaiian achievement. This volume documents the political and cultural history of the sacred island of Mokuʻula and the ongoing efforts of the Lahaina community to recover and preserve this special place of Native Hawaiian heritage.

The Native Hawaiian Culture and Arts Program (NHCAP) was created by the U.S. Congress through the American Indian, Alaska Native, and Native Hawaiian Culture and Arts Development Act (Higher Education Amendments of 1986, P. L. 99-498). It was implemented in 1987 upon the execution of the first cooperative agreement between the National Park Service and Bishop Museum. NHCAP is dedicated to making a meaningful and continuing contribution to the well-being of Native Hawaiian people through the perpetuation and growth of Native Hawaiian language, culture, arts, and values.

W. Donald Duckworth
President and Director, Bishop Museum
Vice Chairman, Board of Trustees, Native Hawaiian Culture and Arts Program

Moku'ula

Maui's Sacred Island

P. Christiaan Klieger

Bishop Museum Press
Honolulu, Hawai'i
1998

Library of Congress Cataloging-in-Publication Data

Klieger, P. Christiaan.
    Moku'ula : Maui's sacred island / P. Christiaan Klieger.
        p.   cm.
    Includes bibliographical references (p.) and index.
    ISBN 1-58178-002-8
    1. Moku'ula (Lahaina, Hawaii)   2. Sacred space--Hawaii--Lahaina.
3. Islands--Hawaii--Lahaina.   4. Lahaina (Hawaii)--History.
5. Hawaii--Religious life and customs.   I. Title.
DU629.L33K55   1998
996.9' 21--dc21   98-31620

To Patrick

Contents

Figures and Tables   viii

Preface   ix

Acknowledgments   xi

Chapter 1. **Introduction**   1
In the Land of the Red Mists   1
Centering   3

Chapter 2. **Descent from the Gods**   7
The Mo'o Arrives in Hawai'i   7
Worship of Kihawahine   10
Children of Kihawahine   15
The Wars of Unification   18
Sacred Children of the Unified Kingdom   22

Chapter 3. **Queen Keōpūolani Returns Home**   25
New Homes, New Influence   26
Death of the Great Queen   28
Pā Halekamani   32
Traditional Religion and Christianity in the Late 1820s   36

Chapter 4. **Kamehameha III Rules from Moku'ula**   39
Breaking the New Kapu   40
A Tomb and Residence Established at Moku'ula   45
Kekāuluohi, the "Big-Mouth Queen"   51
The Royal Court of Lahaina in the Early 1840s   52
Kalua'ehu and the Great Mahele   58
Wedges, Circles, Sacred Boundaries, and Legal Wrangling   69
Maui Departure   72
The Last Resort   76

Chapter 5. **Ghost Island**   79
The Death of Kamehameha III   79
Moku'ula in the 1850s and 1860s   81
Continuing Debates over Land Tenure   87
The Demise of the Tomb at Moku'ula   93
The Filling of Loko o Mokuhinia   94
The Future   98

Appendix. **Archaeological Excavations at Moku'ula**   101

Notes   111

Index   121

Figures and Tables

Figures

1	King Kamehameha III's royal palace in Lahaina in the early 1840s	3
2	Moku'ula within the context of modern Lahaina	4
3	Lahaina fishponds	6
4	Drawing of a statue (ki'i) of Kihawahine or Lailai	11
5	Carved tooth, possibly representing a mo'o head	13
6	Genealogical relationships of kings of Maui to Kihawahine	16
7	Lamentations for Keōpūolani	29
8	King Kamehameha III, 1825	34
9	Halekamani	36
10	Princess Nāhi'ena'ena	40
11	King Kamehameha III as a young man	41
12	Ulumaheiheihoapili in 1837	47
13	Timothy Ha'alilio, ca. 1830s	47
14	Auhea Miriam Kekāuluohi, 1845	51
15	Presbyterian Church, Lahaina, 1851	59
16	Monsarrat sketch of Moku'ula area, late 1840s	60
17	Possible view of Shaw Street, 1856	61
18	Lower Waine'e ahupua'a in the 1840s	62
19	Sociopolitical relationships and the Lahaina landscape	70
20	Keoni Ana, or John Young II, ca. 1850	74
21	King's summer home on O'ahu, 1853	75
22	Queen Kalama, ca. 1850	76
23	Kamehameha III	76
24	Funeral of King Kamehameha III, 1855	80
25	Fanny Young Na'ea, ca. 1860	85
26	Map of Lahaina, ca. 1860	86
27	Ruth Ke'elikōlani	88
28	Possible site of Alice Shaw Ka'ae's home, Loko o Nalehu, Waiokama	89
29	Shaw Street, looking east, 1910	92
30	Enroachment of canefields around the beachfront of Lahaina, ca. 1930	95
31	Hale pili of a commoner family in Lahaina, ca. 1890	95
32	Loko o Mokuhinia with sedge banks, ca. 1894–97	96
33	Loko o Mokuhinia, ca. 1897–1913	97
34	Lahaina fishpond, possibly Loko o Mokuhinia, ca. 1890	98
35	Malu'ulu o Lele Park and archaeological site map, Lahaina	102
36	Deposition rates, radiocarbon assays, and stratigraphic levels, Core 7	104
37	Moku'ula pier structure	110

Tables

1	Royal burials at Halekamani	45
2	Selected kuleana of Pākalā, Lahaina, Maui	66
3	Kuleana of the Crown, ahupua'a of Waine'e, Lahaina, Maui	67
4	Selected kuleana of Waiokama, Lahaina, Maui	68
5	Probable burials at tomb on Moku'ula	82

Preface

Mokuʻula in Lahaina is an *axis mundi* of the Hawaiian world. Here political rule and religious ritual operated in concert, from the days of the emergence of the Maui kingdom, through the unification of the Islands and then the coming of Christianity, to the modern age. During the twentieth century, however, this Maui vicinity witnessed the loss of native rule and the physical conversion of the sacred precincts into a public baseball field. Despite this fact, Mokuʻula has remained a place set apart, generation after generation, to the present day. This is the story of that continuity.

Mokuʻula was the locale of the private residential complex of Kauikeaouli, King Kamehameha III of the Hawaiian Islands, from 1837 to 1845—those years when Lahaina was the capital of the Hawaiian kingdom. The residence was constructed on a tiny island in a freshwater fishpond, Loko o Mokuhinia. The site was religiously significant to the old Maui royal family, having been a home of their tutelary deity, the lizard goddess Kihawahine. The location was important to Kamehameha III, born a living god and descended from both Maui and Hawaiʻi royal families. Also within the Mokuʻula complex is the site of the Lahaina palace of the great King Piʻilani, the sixteenth-century unifier of the kingdom of Maui.

This book places Mokuʻula within the political geography of Lahaina and the island of Maui. The story of the sacred island explores the significance of the lizard goddess in Native Hawaiian culture and her relationship to the fishpond surrounding Mokuʻula. The unification of Maui under Piʻilani, his residence at the site, and the deification of his daughter as lizard goddess to dwell in the surrounding fishpond are the mythic core of this history.

The genealogical "concentration" of royal Maui blood, symbolized by the power of the lizard goddess, is a theme in the struggle for supremacy over all the Hawaiian Islands by the Maui kings. When Kamehameha I of the Big Island of Hawaiʻi emerged victorious, he adopted the Maui royal family, its gods, and its sacred sites in their entirety. Mokuʻula itself became a center for the entire island chain, and Kamehameha's son Kauikeaouli chose to reign as Kamehameha III from this tiny, sacred island. Here he buried beloved members of his family and lived with his queen in secure isolation.

As the growing city of Honolulu eventually overshadowed little Lahaina, the royal court reluctantly moved to Oʻahu in 1845. Without its *aliʻi* and Native Hawaiian guardians, Mokuʻula began a slow slip into obscurity. Eventually the island and fishpond were filled in and converted for use as a recreational area. Archaeological work in 1993 rediscovered the site of Mokuʻula buried under Maluʻulu o Lele Park and provided other information regarding the founding of the village of

Lahaina. A summary of conclusions from these archaeological excavations is attached as an Appendix to this book.

The story of Moku'ula tells of a royal Hawaiian court during a protracted and anxious period of cultural transformation. From rule by virtue of divine sanction to that of Western-introduced constitutional government, a pattern of behavior clearly emerges in Kamehameha III that is substantially different from missionary and missionary-influenced scholarly accounts of his life. The profile of Kamehameha III, inscribed as it is on the islet of Moku'ula, suggests a monarch tormented by conflicting interests: upholding traditional Native Hawaiian practices while sincerely considering the values and innovations brought forward by foreigners. I suggest that one symptom of this conflict was Kauikeaouli's demonstrated need for privacy and retreat, and that the establishment of the private residence at Moku'ula was one means to satisfy this requirement. To know Kamehameha III and his royal Maui genealogy is to know the reason for Moku'ula. And to know a bit about the tiny island of Moku'ula is to understand the spirit of Maui.

The phenomenon of Moku'ula is a Hawaiian illustration of the fact that many powerful sacred sites throughout the world are notable simply because they persist. Immediately prior to beginning work on this book in 1993, I had the fortune to spend time at the Gothic cathedral of Saint-Denis just outside Paris. This was the ancient burial site of the kings of France and the place of martyrdom of the patron saint of that city. Deep within the royal crypt, across from the sarcophagi of Louis XVI and Marie Antoinette, is a large open chamber. Looking down into the gloom, I could see successive layers of church foundations. Back through the Dark Ages to the early Christian era, nested shells of prior church groundwork provide evidence of a continual demarcation of the hallowed earth at the site. Near the center of the ruins lies the remains of a Roman temple. No doubt the locale of Saint-Denis was sacred to the pre-Roman Gauls as well. Here was the mystic center of the people of Paris, of the Île de France, and of the greater nation—attended to, adorned, rebuilt, and reconsecrated throughout the entire span of recorded history. Despite the religious, linguistic, and political differences emerging and fading throughout that enormous course of human experience, the site has remained sacred to the present day.

P. Christiaan Klieger
San Francisco, 1998

Acknowledgments

The author thanks the staff of the Lahaina Restoration Foundation for providing generous access to their archives at Hale Paʻi. Valuable materials were also provided by Lori Sablas and Akoni Akana of the Poʻokela staff of Kāʻanapali Beach Hotel. The County of Maui Cultural Resources Commission and Poʻokela are thanked for conceiving the archaeological research project and securing funding. Elizabeth Anderson and Brian Miskae of the County Planning Department provided many resources for the study of Mokuʻula, and their assistance is greatly appreciated. Funding for this book's publication has been provided by the Bishop Museum Native Hawaiian Culture and Arts Program (NHCAP), through a Cooperative Agreement with the National Park Service, U.S. Department of the Interior.

I am particularly happy to have received guidance, encouragement, and *aloha* from *kūpuna* Pua and Ned Lindsey, Mildred Kaʻahane, Aunties Sarah and Nani, and other holders of the oral legacy of Mokuhinia and Lahaina. No intrusion into this sacred site could have been made without their supervision, knowledge, and skill. Among the many who have been instrumental in this project are *kahu* Kekapa Lee of Waiola Church, Keola Sequira, Pam Colorado, William Waiʻohu, and the Friends of Mokuʻula. Very special aloha goes to Noni Shaw-Mirchovich, who is tied by bonds of blood to this land and its story.

At Bishop Museum, acknowledgment goes to the great editorial staff at Bishop Museum Press, the members of the Archives and Library, and my colleagues at the Department of Anthropology. Special thanks to John Thomas, editor of this book.

Thanks especially to Stephan D. Clark, Dr. Boyd Dixon, and Dr. Susan A. Lebo for their advice throughout the project. Thanks for the ideas, Ignatz, the patience, Patrick, and the faith, Nathan!

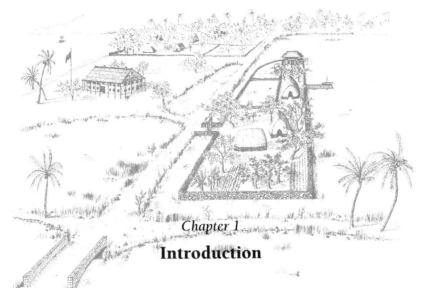

Chapter 1

Introduction

Moku'ula is a story of a royal palace and ancient religious site nearly lost in the maelstrom of a rapidly changing Hawaiian culture. Moku'ula was once a one-acre island set in a large, freshwater fishpond in the Maui community of Lahaina—it now lies underneath a baseball park. The site, built over the grotto of a protector goddess, was an archaic seat of the Maui kings. In the nineteenth century, the small moated island of Moku'ula was graced with the private apartments of King Kamehameha III, son of Kamehameha the Great, set within a larger palace complex. From this tiny, sacred island the unified Hawaiian kingdom was ruled.

As well as being the site of a nineteenth-century royal palace, Moku'ula was a sanctuary for *ali'i,* a place of *kapu*—even after the so-called downfall of the indigenous Hawaiian religion in 1819. A place set apart, Moku'ula was a locus upon which the realms of spirit, land, and human politics intersected.

In the Land of the Red Mists

Moku'ula's function in Native Hawaiian tradition and its importance as a residence for *ali'i nui* (paramount rulers) can be inferred from the meaning of the name Moku'ula. A *moku* is a division of land, an island, something that is separate or cut.[1] *'Ula* is one of those complex Hawaiian words possessing manifold meanings, elaborate connotations, and poetic possibilities. *'Ula* may simply refer to the color red, the redness of the volcanic soils of the island; or it may signify sacred and royal, red being the royal color, the color of life and fire. *'Ula* may also mean ghost or spirit.

From the legends, myths, and documented history of Moku'ula, it appears that all three major meanings are appropriate to this special place. It is an island set apart, physically and socially; the soils of Moku'ula are indeed bright red; the island was used for *ali'i nui* residence and probably religious ritual; a known burial location, Moku'ula is to this day considered by some to be inhabited by a guardian spirit in the form of a lizard (*'aumakua mo'o*).

According to legend, Moku'ula was the traditional Kalua o Kiha, the grotto of the highest *mo'o* goddess, Kihawahine, who swam in the surrounding Loko o Mokuhinia.[2] Historically, the strip of land on the beach side of Moku'ula was the site of the palace of the unifier of the Maui kingdom, Pi'ilani, from the sixteenth century.

It is speculated that the emergent importance of Moku'ula as focus, or *piko,* for Native Hawaiian religion and state ideology was enhanced by the strategic usefulness of Lahaina during the wars of interisland unification of the eighteenth century. It is known, for example, that the goddess Kihawahine was frequently evoked by Kamehameha I during his conquest of the Hawaiian Islands. The axis of this assessment of Lahaina was based on ancient Polynesian concepts of religion and statecraft. By the time Kamehameha I arrived at the West Maui community, Moku'ula was already of legendary importance to Native Hawaiians.

With the death of King Kamehameha I in 1819, the *kapu* system of proprietary restrictions, the pillar of the traditional Native Hawaiian religion, was abolished. This radical act, initiated without the direct influence of foreign Christian missionaries, is a hallmark in the study of culture change. When missionaries arrived from Boston the following year, they were met with the convenience of a indigenous people "without religion." But in the years to follow, while new Christian churches were being erected upon former *heiau* and wooden images of the gods were being put to the torch, the sacred island of Moku'ula continued along its original path as a royal sanctuary for the king.

In the 1830s and 1840s, Moku'ula became the private residence of King Kamehameha III and his court. The island remained an umbilicus for the unified Hawaiian kingdom. There was a tomb for the king's beloved mother, sister, children, and other royal family members on the island from 1837 to 1884. In a sense, the old *kapu* held at Moku'ula—the powers of the Christian mission, the foreign businessmen and transients, and the Christianized *ali'i* had little effect upon the king's sanctuary.

A sprawling coral block palace, Hale Piula, was constructed fronting the beach at this location in the 1840s but was never taken seriously as a residence by either the king or his subjects. The fishpond of Mokuhinia, with its small island, was immediately in the rear (*mauka*) of Hale Piula; this was the true residence of the king. The private apartments and the royal family's mausoleum on the island were linked to the formal, Western-style palace by a gated causeway. Security, privacy, and sanctity were the major themes of Kamehameha III's residence on Moku'ula (Figure 1).

Figure 1. King Kamehameha III's royal palace in Lahaina in the early 1840s, based on historical and archaeological evidence. Hale Piula is seen to the left. The tomb is at the far end of Moku'ula, with a pier and *hale pili* nearer the center of the island. The intersection of Shaw and Fronts Streets is in the foreground. Among other features, archaeological excavations in 1993 discovered the remains of the pier, the island retaining wall, and a holding pond. Author's reconstruction.

From this spot, King Kamehameha III chose to rule. Residence at Moku'ula was for him an unimpeachable source of traditional legitimacy and solace during a period of great change in the Hawaiian kingdom. It continued as such until the capital was moved to Honolulu in 1845. Recently, the island has again become the focus of Native Hawaiian sovereignty deliberations, as Maui citizens weigh the overlapping values of historic preservation and public recreation. Moku'ula, it could be said, is an island of continuity. Its contemporary significance is drawn from the gravity of history and from the fact that this site, among the most important in Hawai'i, was nearly forgotten. Moku'ula has now recaptured the imagination of new generations of Hawaiians.[3]

Centering

The site of the royal palace at Lahaina is two to three feet below the surface of a county baseball park in the south section of town, immediately north of Front Street at Shaw (Figure 2). No remains of the palace compound are visible on the surface. The general neighborhood around Moku'ula is presently that of a small

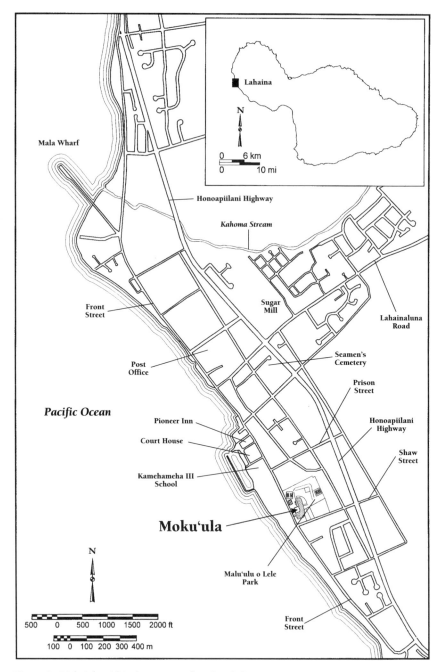

Figure 2. Moku'ula within the context of modern Lahaina.

urbanized resort, with multistory hotels, fast-food outlets, and numerous T-shirt shops existing alongside quaint, plantation-style single-family residences, parking lots, and open fields. Lahaina, on the coast of West Maui, is itself strategically located near the geographic center of the six major inhabited Hawaiian islands.

The site of the palace compound is presently bisected on the west by Front Street, which even in the days of Kamehameha III separated the Hale Piula palace from the Moku'ula residences. Mokuhinia Street is to the north and Shaw Street to the south, and an old stone wall to the east demarcates the property of Waiola Church. Early documents suggest that Mokuhinia fishpond was considerably larger than the 11 acres recorded in the early nineteenth century, extending to perhaps 17 acres.

The island of Moku'ula was in a freshwater, spring-fed fishpond that formed naturally behind a long beach berm. Moku'ula was about 100 meters east of the mean coastal stand. Its elevation was only about one meter above mean sea level. The topography of the surface of the present-day park is nearly flat, exhibiting only about 20–30 centimeters of elevational variance throughout the region.

Much of the site of the palace complex is within the traditional *ahupua'a* of Waine'e. *Ahupua'a* were traditional, semiautonomous land divisions that usually extended from the sea to the mountains, radiating in wedge-shape fashion from some high ridge or crest. Containing natural resources from many environments, *ahupua'a* were recognized as the primary sociopolitical land division in old Hawai'i. Hale Piula, Loko o Mokuhinia, and the northern half of Moku'ula were in Waine'e, and the southern half of the island and some adjoining fishponds were in the *ahupua'a* of Waiokama (as adjudicated in the 1870s). Waine'e *ahupua'a* extended from the shoreline at Lahaina to a point on the 1,000 foot USGS contour just north of the mountain rivulet known as Kaua'ula Stream.

Superimposed over the ancient Lahaina *ahupua'a* system during the residence of the kings was a pattern of nested circles. In the center was the sacred island of Moku'ula, the home of the highest *ali'i nui*. It was surrounded by the fishpond Mokuhinia, the "pit of Kiha." Kalua o Kiha was in turn enveloped by Kalua'ehu, the chiefly region of Lahaina. Beyond this circle lived the *maka'āinana*, the commoners of West Maui. The highly stratified royal Hawaiian sociopolitical system was thus replicated in the ordering of the Lahaina landscape.

Kalua'ehu was "the pit of the red-head," a reference to an auburn-haired *mo'o* lizard goddess. The term also could mean the land of the "many and colorful," a reference to the chiefs in their resplendent featherwork. Kalua'ehu was bordered on the north by Pāhumanamana Stream, the present Dickenson Street, and on the south by Kaua'ula Stream, both originally marked by *heiau*. Keawaiki was the name given to an area adjacent to the mouth of Pāhumanamana Stream. To the mountain side, Kalua'ehu extended to the Wao Akua, the divine forest of Mauna

Ke'eke'ehia, and the valleys of Kaua'ula and Launiupoko. The beach of Kalua'ehu is known as Mākila, and the section of surf adjacent to Loko o Mokuhinia is named 'Uo and remembered as a famous surfing area favored by the *ali'i*. Traditionally defined, Kalua'ehu is much larger than the region of the same name known at the time of the Great Mahele land tenure reform of 1848–53.

The fishpond of Mokuhinia lies in a basin at the center of the Kalua'ehu region between Pāhumanamana and Kaua'ula Streams. Loko o Mokuhinia and its sacred island were originally dominated by a coastal wet sedgeland environment of *'aka'akai, aluhā,* and *makaloa* bulrushes. The environment supported by the spring-fed, bedrock pools of Lahaina provided early Native Hawaiians with an abundance of fresh water and shade in an otherwise inhospitable environment. Fish could be stocked in the ponds, and taro could be grown in their shallow precincts. Considering the central location of Lahaina, those that controlled this oasis were powerful indeed (Figure 3).

The freshwater resources of Lahaina, supplying numerous fishponds, taro fields, and lush plantings of sugarcane and other garden produce, have been recognized by countless generations of Native Hawaiians. The bounty of the waters of Lahaina, indeed of Maui, has been symbolically represented from the most distant of mythological times to the present. Upon this enduring symbol, the life of the land and the power of the gods were recognized.

Figure 3. The dark, quiet waters of the Lahaina fishponds. This is most likely a section of Loko o Mokuhinia at the turn of the twentieth century. Bishop Museum CP 77253.

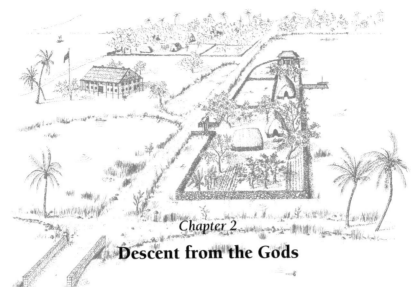

Chapter 2

Descent from the Gods

Now, as in the past, the ubiquitous symbol of Maui is the lizard (mo'o). On T-shirts and key chains sold in every gift shop in Lahaina, the modern *mo'o* appears as a cute, wide-eyed gecko. But the real *mo'o* of this island, its very spirit, is a tremendous female creature who inhabits the depths of several Maui fishponds. She is most closely associated with the sacred island of Moku'ula in Loko o Mokuhinia. More than any other symbol, she represents contemporary Maui in continuity with its royal past.

The Mo'o Arrives in Hawai'i

In traditional Hawaiian religion, the *mo'o* is a black-water apparition, with a long tail and curved back composed of numerous vertebrae—also called *mo'o*. It is possible that it represents a lingering memory of the early Polynesian association with the giant crocodiles or monitor lizards of ancestral Southeast Asia. Each vertebra is a node, connecting the living form of that which goes before it to that which follows. In this sense, the backbone of a *mo'o* is analogous to a genealogy, a succession of people each tied to those who have gone before and those who will follow. The royal *mo'o* of Maui represents the indigenous royal family. She is the backbone that connects the present with the divine ancestors of the past. It was the *mo'o*, as an ancestor, as a guardian, as a representative of the divine lineage, that bound the god-king Kauikeaouli, King Kamehameha III of Maui and the united archipelago, to his sacred *'āina*. The *mo'o* home at Moku'ula makes it the most appropriate locus from which her descendants ruled.

The founding ancestors of the Hawaiian people, Wākea and his half-sister Papa, initially created Hawai'i and Maui islands, according to the famous Kumulipo creation myth.[4] The progenitors also had a human daughter,

Ho'ohōkūikalani. The islands' creation and the daughter's conception were the first example of royal incest, or *pi'o*. The *pi'o* mating system was further elaborated in the reproductive actions of father Wākea and daughter Ho'ohōkūikalani, who mated and gave birth first to the *kalo* (taro) plant and then to a son, Hāloa, the founder of the line of *ali'i nui* and all Hawaiians. These incestuous matings captured the power, the *mana,* of the earth and sky itself. It became desirous for succeeding generations of *ali'i nui* to replicate this act, keeping the *mana* of the creator gods concentrated within this lineage. From Hāloa the son, the Maui royal line descended through the 'Ulu genealogy on its Hema branch.[5] The quest for *pi'o* marriages was especially notable in the Maui royal line and was a source of much of their prestige relative to their sovereign colleagues on other Hawaiian islands. Accomplishing a *pi'o* marriage was a major factor in the life of King Kamehameha III and the final known attempt among the line of paramount rulers descending from Wākea and Papa.

At some point in the highest genealogies of the Hawaiian Islands, the lizard goddess Mo'oinanea arrived from Kahiki (probably Tahiti) with the Kū and Hina families of gods. She had always been associated with the royal Polynesian lineages; the *mo'o* are also gods of the royal Oropa'a family of Tahiti. Inheritance in ancient Hawai'i was bilateral: one could inherit *mana,* affiliation, and property from either the male or female line. The *mo'o* could assume human form; they could possess living humans or deify and reanimate the dead. Symbolizing a living geneaology, *mo'o* quite often became guardians of particular families and lineages, and the task of propitiation fell upon their human descendants. In the Hawaiian Islands, Mo'oinanea was the ancestor of the 'Ulu/Hema lineage of Maui. Mo'oinanea herself appears to have been the highest ranking of the *mo'o,* perhaps the prototype in Hawaiian religion.

In one of her legends, Mo'oinanea lived at Pu'unui, Nu'uanu, O'ahu, in a *lua palolo* (clay pit). In another, she is known for shutting up the "hidden land of Kāne," the mysterious realm where she took care of the gods. One of her descendants was Kelea (Keleanuinoho'ana'api'api), a Maui chiefess and famous surfer who married Kalamakua, a prominent chief on O'ahu. Maui was not yet a unified kingdom at the time, but soon the *mo'o* would be evoked for the unification of the island, and then the entire archipelago. Kelea was a daughter of Kahekili I, the *ali'i nui* of the kingdom of West Maui, and his wife Haukanuimakamaka. The *mo'o* lineage was most likely introduced through Kelea's mother. Kelea's paternal grandfather and great uncle were Kaka'e and Kaka'alaneo, *ali'i nui* of the Wailuku line who ruled West Maui and Lāna'i from Lele/Lahaina in the sixteenth century.[6]

Kelea's brother was Kawaokaohele, who reigned after the death of Kahekili I. His rule was remembered as being quiet, peaceful, and popular. It was during this time that the chiefs of the Hana side (east) of Maui acknowledged the Wailuku lineage as *mōʻī*, paramount chiefs of all Maui, although Kawaokaohele's son Piʻilani generally receives that honor. Kelea's daughter Lāʻieloheloheikawai married her first cousin Piʻilani at Lahaina, the occasion marked by an auspicious red mist over the wide beach of Kāʻanapali.[7]

Piʻilani, Maui's greatest king, is credited with creating a road that encircled the entire island of Maui. Upon this trail the great *mōʻī* made frequent tours throughout the land, collecting taxes during the time of the Makahiki and seeing to general order. He ruled from Lahaina and is known to have died there.[8] His Lahaina residence became associated with the *moʻo* who lived in the adjacent fish-pond of Mokuhinia and guarded his royal family. It is this king and his daughter, who becomes a goddess and lives in the fishpond, that established Mokuʻula as a sacred place for future rulers of Maui and the Hawaiian Islands.

Kihawahine Mokuhinia Kalamaʻula Kalāʻaiheana was the daughter of Piʻilani and Queen Lāʻieloheloheikawai. Kihawahine ("lizard woman") is said to have been born on the birthing stone of Pōhaku Hauola at Mākila beach in the area of the royal *loʻi* (taro fields) known as ʻĀpuakēhau in central Lahaina.[9] Kihawahine's chiefly name, the name that appears in the official genealogies, was Kalāʻaiheana. She was a full sister of kings Lonoapiʻilani and Kihaapiʻilani and of Princess Piʻikea.[10] A double *moʻo* lineage entered Kihawahine through her mother and father (being first cousins descended from Haukanuimakamaka).

Kihawahine lived in the latter part of the sixteenth century. Her brother Kihaapiʻilani became king of Maui, and her sister Piʻikea married the famous chief ʻUmialīloa of Hawaiʻi. Upon her death, the princess was transformed into a *moʻo*, henceforth referred to as Kihawahine Mokuhinia Kalamaʻula. The fishpond associated with her family's residence in Lahaina is thus called Loko o Mokuhinia. Kalamaʻula, Kihawahine, and Mokuhinia sometimes appear to be distinct *moʻo* in Hawaiian history. Kalamaʻula ("Red Torch"), for example, is the name of a place associated with a lizard goddess on Molokaʻi.[11] With high *kapu* members of the Piʻilani family present at Kalamaʻula, Molokaʻi, in the late eighteenth century, it seems likely that the name is synonymous with the goddess Kihawahine.[12]

Famed Hawaiian specialist Mary Kawena Pukui once told historian Dorothy Barrère that the name Kihawahine, referring to Kalāʻaiheana, daughter of Piʻilani, was not mentioned in the genealogies because she was an *ʻeʻepa*—a human born with some sort of supernatural difference. The distinction could be a special mental or physical ability or disability. As a result, *ʻeʻepa* were usually not recorded in mundane genealogy. Such people would often become trickster spirits upon death. Pukui also maintained the legend that Kihawahine Kalāʻaiheana was deified and made a *moʻo* goddess after death, with a home at Mauoni pond on Maui. Kihawahine moved from pond to pond, island to island—she was the only *moʻo* with this ability.

Worship of Kihawahine

Not much is known about the worship of the female *akua,* and particularly of private royal *'aumākua.* The worship of Kihawahine, by her association with the ruling *ali'i,* eventually developed into an instrument of state. Ironically, however, her worship seems to have survived longer than most other forms of Hawaiian religious expression. A clue to its survival past the so-called abolition of traditional Hawaiian religion in 1819 may lie in the fact that *'aumākua* devotion was esoteric and kept secret by the *kahu* (guardians) and family members who had inherited their *'aumākua.*

We do have a few recorded accounts of the characteristics of Kihawahine, and of the rituals and sites associated with her. One can imagine the royal complex at Moku'ula in the days just after the reign of great king Pi'ilani:

> A singularity of Kiha-wahine was her tickly nose. Those chiefs watched over this *mo'o* in the god houses where her keepers worshiped her with offerings of tapa and various other things. The tabu of this sneezer [Kihawahine] was death. There were so many tabus relating to her that it is impossible to speak of them all. Here is one tabu of Kiha-wahine. During the period of the *makahiki* festival (upon the last day), the god Kū'i, the god Pā'ani and all the gods were brought forth. The image of the goddess Kiha-wahine, in all her finery, was then taken aboard a canoe. The paddlemen of this goddess took their places and cried out, announcing that the tabu of this goddess was immediately in effect, as though the goddess herself were actually there. Then the cry proclaiming a tabu on the approach of a sacred personage was announced as follows: "Kapuwō! Kapuwō! Kapuwō! to the tabu of Kiha-wahine. Kapuwō! Death to those who move! Prostrate!" If there were a canoe on the sea at that time, those on the open top of the canoe must prostrate themselves or be killed by the keepers of this goddess. After the goddess passed by, then they would arise and go elsewhere. If they did not act fittingly they were killed.[13]

The *mo'o* had the power to possess her keepers. It was remember by Samuel Kamakau that Kihawahine had such powers:

> Kamehameha relied upon the god Kaho'ali'i who would possess *(noho mai)* this human *kahu* of the god Kaho'ali'i. So also with Kihawahine. She was a female image with hair bleached with lime *(pukai'ia);* and sometimes the image of Kihawahine was decorated with *olena* [a turmeric] and *puaniu* [coconut blossom] and *pokohukohu* [noni root] tapas. This image was only a symbol. The spirit of Kihawahine would possess a man *(noho 'uhane),* or if not, she showed herself in some awesome and terrifying god form *(kino akua).* So it was with others of Kamehameha.[14]

A representation of Kihawahine (or Lailai) was discovered in 1885 at Waimanu, Hawaiʻi, and drawn by Robert C. Barnfield (Figure 4). The back of this image's head was once decorated with hair or feathers, and the eyes were inlaid with pearl shell. Human teeth lined the mouth. Still, the images (kiʻi) of the goddess were only that; the real Kihawahine was represented through her family or in one of her manifold physical forms.

John Papa ʻĪʻī, a courtier in the retinue of King Kamehameha I, described a major ritual dealing with the female deities held in conjunction with long dedication ceremonies, or loulu, at heiau luakini (temples of human sacrifice) and their associated hale o Papa, women's temples dedicated to the earth goddess, Papa. In the ceremony, two goddess images, Kalamainuʻu/Kihawahine and Haumea, were wrapped in turmeric-dyed tapa and their images were set up in the hale o Papa. In one traditional tale, Kalamainuʻu had lost an eye in her battle with Haumea, and this was depicted in her image.[15] At the very end of the kapu loulu ceremony, "the women at the head of the kingdom" presented fine tapas, dog, and other food offerings on the altars of the goddesses. The highest women of state officiated at these ceremonies of offering and propitiation to Kihawahine and Haumea.[16]

Figure 4. Drawing of a statue (kiʻi) of Kihawahine or Lailai by Robert C. Barnfield (1855–93). The image was found by Native Hawaiians at Waimanu, Oʻahu, in 1885. Bishop Museum CP 76846.

On a more familial level of *moʻo* worship, we have some idea of the appropriate offerings to one's *ʻaumakua:*

> If the *ʻaumakua* is a *moʻo*, they get a reddish-brown dog, or a brown one, or a mottled one, or a dog with a spot on each jowl, or one striped like a caterpillar, or a brindled dog, and whatever the persons directing them say in the way of tapas—a saffron yellow tapa (*ʻolena*), or a light yellow one (*he māhuna*), or one the color of ripening *hala* fruit (*he halakea*), or one the color of the blossom of the coconut (*he kapa pua niu*)—and other things, including a whole *ʻawa*, and wrap all the sacrifices in a striped tapa (*kapa moelua*). Then, when all is quiet (*noho a hano ka leo*), they take the bundle to a pond fed by springs and hide it in the water.[17]

Thus we see the offering of dog in both state and familial *ʻaumakua* rituals. The rites described here are most likely in reference to the *moʻo* of Loko o Mokuhinia, a "pond fed by springs." Moses Manu made a further association between Loko o Mokuhinia and Kihawahine, noting a more universalistic character of her worship:[18]

> This moo Kihawahine was a moo on whom the parents of these chiefs relied and the place where Kihawahine lived was in a pond lying at Lahaina, Maui, by the name of Mokuhinia. The location of the tomb of the chiefess (Princess) Nahienaena, which stood in the pond on the east bank, was Mokuula, a little rock island. Below this was the den of this moo. This hole was called, from ancient times until this day, Ka-lua-o-Kiha (The Den of Kiha).
>
> This was the lizard that had the greatest number of caretakers and many worshippers to deify it. Chiefs and commoners worshiped it all over Maui, Molokai and Lanai in ancient times and to it belongs the pit in the pond of Mokuhinia in Lahaina. Look at the story of Kiha-a-Piilani.... It was said ... that Kihawahine made a circuit of Maui and also of Hawaii, Oahu, and Kauai. In this journey there were many worshippers from Hawaii and Niihau. It was the only lizard that went around the islands of the group.

In archaeological investigations at a Lahaina houselot on the northeast shoreline of the former Loko o Mokuhinia, a small carved tooth excavated near the site of chief Pikanele's early nineteenth-century residence looks very much like the head of a gecko (Figure 5). Could this be an image of Kihawahine?

The one-and-the-many aspect of the *moʻo* is a recurring theme. The multiplicity of her forms reflects the symbolism of myriad vertebrae forming a single spine. Kamakau relates:

Kalamainuʻu, Laniwahine, Hauwahine, Kanekuaʻana, and Kihawahine, and the myriads (kini a me ka lehu) of interchangeable body forms (kino lau) of the moʻo (water spirits) used to be worshiped constantly. Persons would be transfigured to become such strange beings (kino ʻeʻepa), but it was not done by merely being buried along a stream or river or beside a spring or having their bones thrown into the water. If they were not related to the moʻo … they had no rightful place, kuleana, in the kino lau of the moʻo…. Akua moʻo were kept for … the health and welfare of the people, and to bring them fish.[19]

The home of the moʻo was kapu to all but her descendants. In life as well as in death, Mokuʻula was home to the family of Kihawahine, the Maui royal family. The lizard herself might not always be at home. The suggestion of kino lau, the myriad of interchangeable forms, again indicates that Kihawahine was not necessarily exclusively associated with Loko o Mokuhinia. The fishpond of Haneoʻo in Hāna District, Maui, was also thought to be Kihawahine's home.[20] As mentioned earlier, she seems to have resided at Kalamaʻula, Molokaʻi, and she was even found on Kauaʻi.

W. C. Bennett described a heiau dedicated to a Kihawahine found on Niʻihau by J. F. G. Stokes in 1912. This structure, found on the beach at Pali Koaʻe, Lehua, functioned as a puʻuhonua (place of refuge) as well as a temple. It was a rectangular enclosure, about 16 by 90 feet, with walls 3 feet wide and 5 to 6 feet high. Along the outer wall, a bench about 1 foot high encircled the perimeter, and there was an 8-foot wide entrance on the inland side.[21] Was this Kihawahine the same as the moʻo associated with the family of Maui's Piʻilani?

The mouth of Hālawa Stream in ʻEwa District, Oʻahu, was once similar to Mokuhinia pond's mythic landscape. Here, we have more recent clues to the ancient worship of the moʻo. At Hālawa, freshwater ponds were guarded by moʻo in the center of the ahupuaʻa. The mouth of the stream might have possessed a koʻa shrine dedicated to the deity.[22] The freshwater ponds of ʻEwa District were generally guarded by the lizard Kānekuaʻana. Rather than being a royal moʻo, however, she was the kiaʻi, the guardian of the makaʻāinana of the district. A deified ancestress, Kānekuaʻana was propitiated by the people of the land during times of scarcity of fish. They erected heiau and presented cooked offerings to bring about the blessings of the moʻo upon the people. In legend, Kānekuaʻana had brought

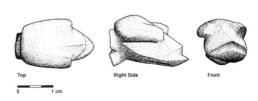

Figure 5. Carved tooth, possibly representing a moʻo head, found in excavations near Pikanele's house site (LCA 310.3) on the shoreline of Loko o Mokuhinia.

the *pipi* (oyster) from Kahiki to the 'Ewa lochs, and she took them away as well when the *kapu* surrounding their harvesting was broken in the 1850s. Similar to the behavior of Kihawahine, the 'Ewa *mo'o* would possess her female descendants. One old woman who was the medium of Kānekua'ana was caught harvesting *pipi* and was punished by the local *konohiki*. The *mo'o* was angry at the greed of the landlords and the abuse leveled at her descendant—the goddess took the pearl oyster back to Kahiki. *Mo'o* tales were repeated throughout the nineteenth century at Pearl Harbor and continued well into the twentieth century.

As the *mo'o* forms were malleable, so too does it appear that their association with specific places was not fixed and immutable. They were active, chthonic spirits of the springs and fresh waters, and they flowed as the water itself. Kihawahine traveled to all the islands; she was not fixed to any one locus. Her behavior was reflected, or mimicked, in the practice of the ancient *ali'i nui,* who, for the purposes of support and taxation, generally were not attached to any one place. In the case of the royal *mo'o* Kihawahine, it appears that wherever she resided so too did the apparatus of state, and vice versa.

The kingdom that propitiated ancestral *mo'o* prospered; those *haku 'āina* or *konohiki* (landlords) that exploited the ponds at the expense of the *maka'āinana* of that place were often punished.[23] The known places of worship of the *mo'o* Kihawahine were *hale puaniu,* the coconut flower temples associated with *ali'i nui* at the largest temple complexes; *hale o Papa,* temples for women built as an adjunct to the exclusively male *heiau luakini;* and smaller *ko'a,* which could be dedicated to *mo'o* guardians of freshwater fishponds as well as to the gods of saltwater fishing. If there was a shrine to the *mo'o* on Moku'ula, it was most likely a *hale puaniu,* an *ali'i*-built structure dedicated to the *'aumakua* adjacent to the king's palace. According to Kamakau, a *hale puaniu* was a house set apart *(moku hale)* within an enclosure. Within, offerings of yellow tapa dyed with *'olena* or *noni* were made to the *mo'o,* as were prodigious quantities of *'awa.* The officiant at the *hale puaniu* was the *kahu mo'o.* The *mo'o* would appear in the waters and would be fed *'awa* and red, brown, or mottled dog cooked in the *imu.* Since the traditional court was transient, the *hale puaniu* and images of Kihawahine and the other deities probably accompanied the entourage on their circuits. The *akua kahu* would reside wherever the court was. The *mo'o* herself was as flexible, transient, and ephemeral as any of the *ali'i nui* in their traditional wanderings.

In the traditional burial ritual, bones of the deceased destined to be transformed would be taken away by the *mo'o.* The dead could assume one of the many bodies of the *'aumakua,* in a manner similar to Kihawahine, who also had the ability to possess her living family members *(ke'ehi pa'a).* The *'ohana* could then gaze upon the *mo'o* if they wished. From these manifold spirits and powers issued the *kapu ho'ola'a,* the *kapu* of consecration. Contact with objects and people so sanctified would be forbidden to those not related to the 'aumakua, and illness could plague transgressors. This is the source of the *kapu* of the tiny island of Moku'ula.

Loko o Mokuhinia was a location highly appropriate for the erection of a *heiau* for symbolic geopolitical reasons in addition to its historic association with Pi'ilani and the Kihawahine lineage. Major religious structures in the Hawaiian Islands were often established on boundaries between political units, especially between *ahupua'a* that were traditionally defined by watersheds. The isle of Moku'ula lies not only at the center of the royal establishment of Kalua'ehu but also precisely on the border between the historically known *ahupua'a* of Waine'e and Waiokama. Moku'ula was a thus a center and a border simultaneously. It had a rich potential for sacred ascription due to this liminal nature as a boundary.[24] Furthermore, Moku'ula expressed social liminality by its physical separation from other land by the encompassing waters of Loko o Mokuhinia.

A *ko'a* or similar shrine placed on Moku'ula would have served as a religio-political boundary marker in the manner that *pōhaku*, large *heiau*, or *ahu pua'a* ("pig altars") functioned elsewhere in Hawai'i. Typically, *ahu pua'a* were placed on the seaward boundary between political divisions,[25] and the people of the land would place their tribute to the *ali'i* on these altars during the Makahiki festival.

Children of Kihawahine

Despite her *'e'epa* status, the daughter of Pi'ilani, Princess Kihawahine Kalā'aiheana, is not obscure by any means. She is found in at least two traditional genealogies, and these indicate that the goddess left many royal descendants. In the first generation, Kihawahine Kalā'aiheana mated with Kamalama and gave birth to Nihoa Kamalama. Subsequently, Nihoa Kamalama mated with Kuihewakanaloahano to have three daughters, Kualu, Kahakumaka, and Maluna.[26] The Maluna line produced many notable *ali'i*, including the last king and queen regnant of the Hawaiian Islands, Kalākaua and his sister Lili'uokalani (Figure 6).

The Maui royal family descended from Pi'ilani was notable in the archipelago for carefully maintaining and replicating *mana* through the *kapu* system and through brother-sister *(pi'o)* or other closely related matings, in imitation of the creative passions of Papa and Wākea. This marriage pattern was especially frequent in the eighteenth century, resulting in great prestige for the Maui line. The power generated by several generations of *pi'o* matings by the sacred members of the Pi'ilani family and the restrictions associated with their *kapu* made the family's dignity, ascribed authority, and status practically unrivaled among the *ali'i nui* of the Hawaiian Islands. The *pi'o* system served to concentrate the *mana* of the gods within the ruling class.[27] Especially important was the power of the guardian Kihawahine among the Maui royal family, a symbol of the family's *mana*.

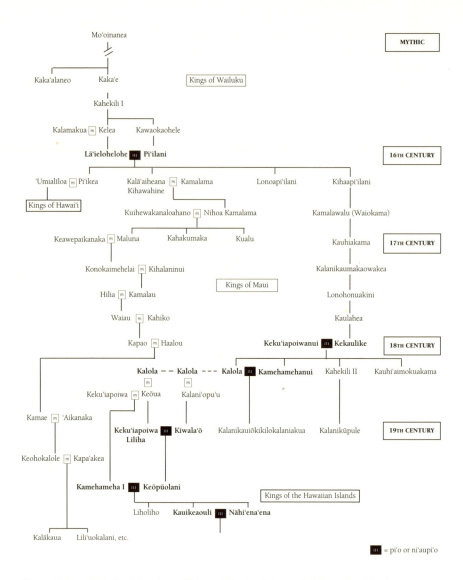

Figure 6. Genealogical relationships of kings of Maui and the unified Hawaiian Islands to Kihawahine.

Seven lineal generations of descent from Pi'ilani, Kekaulike became *mō'ī* of Maui in the early eighteenth century. His *nī'aupi'o*[28] children included King Kamehamehanui, who built the important Wailehua *heiau* to the south of Loko o Mokuhinia in Lahaina, at the mouth of Kaua'ula Stream, around A.D. 1738. The construction of the religious structure was not a popular project, however, and the people of Lahaina rioted. The fabrication of the temple was an escalating cause for intrafraternal warfare between Kamehamehanui and his elder brother Kauhiʻaimokuakama. The feud became a conflict that eventually brought in the ruling chiefs Alapaʻinui of Hawaiʻi and Peleioholani of Oʻahu. This war brought great destruction to the food-producing resources of Lahaina. In later years, the stones of the temple of Wailehua would provide a tomb for Kamehamehanui's grandniece, Keōpūolani, sacred wife of Kamehameha I.[29]

Kekaulike was the *hānai* father of the celebrated *kapu* twins depicted on the royal Hawaiian coat of arms. One of the twins, Kameʻeiamoku, was the father of Ulumaheiheihoapili (Hoapili), a close friend of Kamehameha I. Resident of Loko o Mokuhinia, Hoapili was the last *kahu* of Kihawahine before the arrival of Christian missionaries.

Another son of Kekaulike was the great King Kahekilinuiʻahumanu (Kahekili II, "The Thunder"), the empire builder who eventually ruled several islands at the center of the Hawaiian Archipelago.[30] He was known to have sacrificed to Kihawahine and was renowned for being tattooed over half his body. Kahekili II was considered so sacred that whatever had touched his body was burned with fire. In 1783, he won the island of Oʻahu and its vassal Molokaʻi in battle. His reputation as a cruel opponent was notorious; he even roasted defeated chiefs in the *imu*. Kahekili II was the reputed father of Kamehameha I.

Kekaulike's daughter Kalola Pupuka possessed many *kapu* and probably carried the power of Kihawahine. Kalola's daughter by her full brother Kamehamehanui was the stratospheric *piʻo* chiefess Kalanikauiōkikilokalaniakua. She was described by Fornander as one "who in those days was one of the highest tabu chiefs, on whom the sun was not permitted to shine, and who, unless with extraordinary precautions, only moved about when the sun was so low as not to throw its beams upon her head."[31] These precautions were necessary because *aliʻi* of the highest *kapu,* such as Kalanikauiōkikilokalaniakua, had the dreaded *kapu moe* (taboo of prostration):

> If the shadow of a man fell upon the house of a tabu chief, that man must be put to death, and so with any one whose shadow fell upon the back of the chief, or upon his robe or *malo,* or upon anything that belonged to the chief…. When a tabu chief ate, the people in his presence must kneel, and if any one raised his knee from the ground, he was put to death. A chief who had the *kapu-moe*—as a rule—went abroad only at night; but if he travelled in daytime a man went before him with a flag calling out *"kapu! moe!"* whereupon all the people prostrated themselves…. if anyone remained standing, he was put to death. Kiwalao was one of those who had this *kapu moe*.[32]

In a different story, Kalanikauiōkikilokalaniakua is described as being so very *kapu* that even her own children could not eat portions of any food served for her, and no other chief except Keōpūolani could enter her house with a skirt or *malo* on.[33] This was the legacy of Pi'ilani and the source of the prestige accruing to the Maui royal family. Their *mana* was highly coveted by rival, "foreign" chiefs such as Kamehameha of Hawai'i in the eighteenth and early nineteenth centuries.

According to Kamakau, Kihawahine as a *mo'o* also had the *kapu moe*.[34] At times, the divinity of the *kapu* chiefess of Maui and that of the *mo'o* were one and the same.

In addition to Kalanikauiōkikilokalaniakua, the high Maui chiefess Kalola Pupuka gave birth to the *kapu* boy Kīwala'ō by Hawai'i *mo'i* Kalani'ōpu'u. Partly through his maternal descent, Kīwala'ō held the highest status in the Hawai'i royal line. When he matured, he was militarily challenged by Kalani'ōpu'u's nephew, Kamehameha I. Kīwala'ō married his half-sister Keku'iapoiwa Liliha (child of Kalola and Keōua, Kamehameha's father) and brought forth another *nī'aupi'o* chiefess, Keōpūolani. Thus by blood, Keōpūolani would be among the highest in status of both the Maui and Hawai'i royal lines. Her august position, accomplished through her inheritance of the *mana* of Kihawahine and many generations of *pi'o* matings, would glorify any court—and, indeed, her children would rule all the Hawaiian Islands.

Keōpūolani, divine mother of Kauikeaouli, who would reign as King Kamehameha III, was born in 1780 at Pihana in Wailuku, Maui.[35] Even while being raised by a wet nurse, Keōpūolani had such *kapu* that no regular chief or commoner would dare touch or even approach her, lest the transgressor be burned to death. Ironically, she was held to be a compassionate and gentle woman, and it was claimed that no one was put to death on her account. She would become a major prize in the conquest of the Islands by a chief from the south.

The Wars of Unification

There are many reasons Lahaina became a favored place of residence for the *ali'i nui* of the Hawaiian Archipelago. Blessed with natural springs, enhanced with canals and intensive cultivation, the plain of Lahaina was a verdant, productive region. Furthermore, it was located in the center of the island chain along the major canoe routes. It became a keystone in the unification process of the Hawaiian Islands. And Moku'ula, with its rich symbolism, became the holy of holies.

The period of interisland unification in the last half of the eighteenth century witnessed a great amount of destruction throughout much of the settled regions of the archipelago. Hard hit was Lahaina in West Maui. During the struggle between Maui royal brothers Kamehamehanui and Kauhi'aimokuakama, Kamehamehanui's ally Alapaʻinui of Hawaiʻi interrupted the streams of Kauaʻula, Kahana, and Kahoma in the high country above the village, toppled terraces and ʻauwai, and thus destroyed the productive capabilities of the loʻi and fishponds below. The carefully regulated irrigation system of loʻi, ʻauwai, ponds (loko), sluice gates, and embankments dating to at least the days of Piʻilani were soundly destroyed. Being in the center of things did not always bode well for Lahaina.

Lahaina agriculture and aquaculture did not rebound between the numerous battles for interisland supremacy. Years after Alapaʻi's destructive path, Lahaina productivity still seemed marginal, according to the accounts of early Western explorers. Nathaniel Portlock reported in 1786 that West Maui had been devastated by the wars of unification.[36] Lahaina of those days appears to have had little in the way of provisions to offer the passing explorers, perhaps less to feed itself.

In the last decade of the eighteenth century, Kamehameha of Hawaiʻi had set out to conquer all the Hawaiian Islands and to place them under his single rule. No upstart, he nevertheless did not have the hereditary mana of his rivals Kīwalaʻō of Hawaiʻi or the grand Piʻilani lineage of Kahekili II. Any rule established through conquest could be legitimated, however, through the production of offspring with women of the highest possible status surviving among the vanquished.[37] Even if he conquered the Islands, Kamehameha would still need to consolidate rule of the unified islands by producing heirs from the sacred women of the Maui royal family, a well-entrenched family who had already nearly accomplished the unification of the Islands themselves.

Maui and Hawaiʻi forces met in conflict at the famous battle of ʻIao Valley in 1790. Three akua women of Maui, Kalanikauiōkikilokalaniakua, Kekuʻiapoiwa Liliha, and her daughter Keōpūolani, rendezvoused with their sacred elder Kalola Pupuka at Olowalu, south of Lahaina. Together they fled to Molokaʻi and settled in at Kalamaʻula, a holy spot named after their ʻaumakua moʻo, Kihawahine Mokuhinia Kalamaʻula.[38]

Captain George Vancouver provided a late eighteenth-century account of a ravaged Lahaina on his second voyage to the Sandwich Islands in 1793. On 12 March, Vancouver reached Lahaina, where he was met by the very old mōʻī Kahekili II, still ruler of Lānaʻi, Molokaʻi, and Oʻahu. Vancouver recalled that Kamehameha's indecisive battle on Maui devastated Lahaina:[39]

> Attended by our guard and these chiefs, we visited the cultivated parts of the plain of Raheina [Lahaina]; these occupied no very great extent; the part bordering on the sea shore was pleasantly laid out in plantations of taro, potatoes, sugar cane, the cloth plant, & c. tolerable well shaded by spreading trees, chiefly of the breadfruit.… Through these grounds little canals were cut in various directions, that supplied the several planta-

tions with water; the whole originating from a continual spring of excellent water, sufficiently above the level to inundate every part. The taro was growing among the water, but in a very bad state of culture, and in very small quantities. To the ravage and destruction of *Tamaahmaah's* [Kamehameha's] wars, the wretched appearance of their crops was to be ascribed of this they grievously complained, and were continually pointing out the damages they had sustained; the despoiled aspect of the country was an incontrovertible evidence of this melancholy truth. Most of the different tenements in the lands formerly cultivated were now lying waste, their fences partly or intirely broken down, and their little canals utterly destroyed; nor was a hog or a fowl any where to be seen. By far the larger portion of the plain was in this ruinous state; and the small part that was in flourishing condition bore the evident marks of very recent labour.

Vancouver's surgeon Archibald Menzies, however, seemed to indicate that all was not bleak:

On the forenoon of the 17th, I accompanied Captain Vancouver and a party of officers, with the two Niihau women, to see the village of Lahaina, which we found scattered along shore on a low tract of land that was neatly divided into little fields and laid out in the highest state of cultivation and improvement by being planted in the most regular manner with the different esculent roots and useful vegetables of the country, and watered at pleasure by aqueducts that ran here and there along the banks intersecting the fields, and in this manner branching through the greater part of the plantation. These little fields were transplanted in a variety of forms, some in rows, in squares, in clumps and others at random; some according to their nature were kept covered with water, while others were with equal care kept dry by gathering earth around them in little hills. In short, the whole plantation was cultivated with such studious care and artful industry as to occupy our minds and attention with a constant gaze of admiration during a long walk through it, in which we were accompanied by a numerous group of natives that continued very orderly and peaceful the whole time.[40]

Old Kahekili II died later in 1793 at Waikīkī and was succeeded by his son Kalanikūpule, who had been viceroy on Maui while his father ruled from Oʻahu. Kamehameha returned to Lahaina in 1795 with his war fleet and set about plundering the town for basic provisions, with little resistance. In due course he vanquished Kahekili II's son on Maui and continued on to Molokaʻi as part of the long-anticipated invasion of Oʻahu.[41]

On Moloka'i, Kamehameha asked for the sacred daughters of Kalola, which she granted to him upon the condition of her own death. Association with the sacred women of the royal Maui line would of course help Kamehameha consolidate and legitimize his authority in that newly conquered kingdom. As a double bonus, any children born of Kalola's granddaughter Keōpūolani by Kamehameha would tie the senior line of Hawai'i tightly with that of the prestigious Pi'ilani lineage, as it had with Kalola and Kalani'ōpu'u, and Pi'ikea and 'Umi even farther back in time.

Keōpūolani's children by Kamehameha I would be elevated above that of either parent. Inasmuch as Kamehameha's father Keōua was also Keōpūolani's grandfather, Kamehameha was Keōpūolani's uncle. The crossing back of the lineages would provide children who were of the highest *akua* status in the kingdom. Such children would inherit the superior *kapu nī'aupi'o,* the *kapu* of fire (*ahi*), and associations with Kihawahine through their mother. The great chiefess Keōpūolani most likely had the *kapu ho'ola'a* of Kihawahine. So high was Keōpūolani's status that Kamehameha himself had to remove his *malo* (loincloth) in her presence.[42] The *pi'o* marriages, as remembered from the story of Wākea and Papa, were metaphors for creation itself. Through their reproductive mimicry, the *ali'i* class were analogous to the deities as the source of all life.

In obtaining these divine women, Kamehameha naturally adopted the mo'o goddess Kihawahine. She became one of his favorite deities. The conqueror had the powerful war god Kūkā'ilimoku as his "land snatcher," but Kihawahine was one of his "land holders." She represented legitimate authority. Kamehameha took Keōpūolani, Keku'iapoiwa Liliha, and Kalanikauiōkikilokalaniakua from Moloka'i back to Hawai'i, where he established his court at Kailua-Kona. Being captive was not necessarily the wish of these divine women, however. Although Keōpūolani was obedient, the fiery Kalanikauiōkikilokalaniakua despised Kamehameha and did not wish her niece Keōpūolani to sleep with him. Considering her rank superior to all the Hawai'i chiefs, and her own lot insufferable, Kalanikauiōkikilokalaniakua committed suicide in 1808.[43]

Keōpūolani and her mother traveled with Kamehameha to O'ahu in 1795 to be present at the decisive Battle of Nu'uanu Pali, in which Kamehameha defeated the forces of Kalanikūpule. He thus won O'ahu, ruled by Maui kings since 1780. With the exception of Kaua'i, the Hawaiian Islands were now unified under one ruler, King Kamehameha I.

It was actually on O'ahu that an indigenous chief bestowed the name Ke-ōpū-o-lani (The Gathering of Heaven) upon the sacred queen. Her birth name was Ka-lani-kau-i-ka-'alaneo (The Exalted One Placed in the Calm). Keōpūolani was also sometimes known as Wahine Pi'o (Woman of *Pi'o* Rank) as a child.[44]

Sacred Children of the Unified Kingdom

Upon consolidating his rule, Kamehameha appointed governors for his newly conquered islands and returned to Hawai'i to sire offspring of the highest rank. At
Hilo in 1797, Keōpūolani gave birth to her first son, Liholiho. A second child was
premature and died.

In 1802 and 1803, Kamehameha and his court resided in Lahaina. With a
retinue of 1,000, the king built a brick "palace" on the point in front of the present-day public library, surrounded by his court.[45] This was perhaps the first
Western-style building constructed by the *ali'i* in the Hawaiian Islands. Being
poorly fabricated, however, it was only of marginal use as a residence and was
later used for storage. It was here the king declared Liholiho his heir and gave him
the power to consecrate the national *heiau*. Liholiho, now head of the religion,
rededicated Wailehua temple in Lahaina.

In Lahaina the dying state advisor Kame'eiamoku, father of Hoapili, told
Kamehameha that Kahekili II had been his real father. With sorrow, Kamehameha
reflected that his Maui brothers did not have to die after all.[46] The wars of unification nearly over, Kamehameha, in imitation of the great chief Pi'ilani, made major
public improvements to Lahaina: "Walls of taro fields which had been destroyed
in earlier wars were repaired and the rich land was generally made productive
again. Instead of roads they used the little pathways that were formed by the tops
of the stone walls around the taro fields, slightly raised and kept in excellent condition."[47] For the first time, Lahaina was capital of all the Hawaiian Islands, with
the exception of Kaua'i. Kamehameha I encamped here primarily to wait with his
fleet of war canoes (*peleleu*) for the planned invasion of that island. The strategic
location of Lahaina and its fresh water, food, and other resources were again factors in his decision to establish his residence here.

After Lahaina, King Kamehameha I, his queens, heirs, chiefs, warriors, and
servants lived at Waikīkī on O'ahu before moving to Honolulu in 1803. There
they lived in and around the great *heiau* complex of Pākākā. According to 'Ī'ī's recollections of Honolulu in 1810, Kamehameha had established a house for
Kihawahine, Kālaipāhoa, and other gods on the beach at Kuloloia, which was very
near the Pākākā *heiau luakini*.[48] This house may have supplanted the *puaniu* established for Kihawahine at the royal compound at Waikīkī.

In the famous chant "Fallen is the Chief," Kihawahine is mentioned in association with Kamehameha I's adoption of Maui's royal *'aumakua*:

> E Kiha, e Kihawahine mana,
> E Kihawahine mana ia ke po'o 'aumākua,
> (O Kiha, O Kihawahine Supernatural,
> O Kihawahine Supernatural the supreme head of the guardians)

In 1810, King Kaumuali'i of Kaua'i and Ni'ihau peacefully ceded his kingdom to Kamehameha. The unified Kingdom of the Hawaiian Islands was established, and Kihawahine had become an emblem of that union. Her place of deification at the fishpond of Mokuhinia at Lahaina was significant in the ideology of the state and its claim to righteousness (pono). Although Kamehameha I conquered the islands, it was Kihawahine who legitimated his rule. During these early, formative years of the unified kingdom, the highest ranking women of the land—Kalola, Keku'iapoiwa Liliha, Kalanikauiōkikilokalaniakua, and Keōpūolani—were responsible for the worship of Kihawahine in the hale o Papa and puaniu'u.

In 1812, the royal court returned to the island of Hawai'i. The first written reference to Loko o Mokuhinia dates from this time. Gideon La'anui, who grew up in the court of Kamehameha, wrote about the king's return to Hawai'i and stopover in Lahaina: "Capt. Davis had arrived the evening before, so we went ashore to join him & the king. We went with Lalae into the breadfruit grove and ate melons, returning to Keawaiki and had food, after which the king went to Mokuhinia for residence, as did we also. Ipakala was our place." The location of "Ipakala" is not known, but it seems likely that this is Pākalā, the area along the northwest shoreline of Loko o Mokuhinia associated with chiefly residence. A short while after 1812, Kamehameha again stopped at Lahaina and went ashore at Mokuhinia. The king stopped here primarily to collect the ho'okupu (tribute) during the time of the Makahiki.[49]

Kahekilike'eaumoku, a native Maui chief and brother of Kamehameha's wives Ka'ahumanu and Kaheiheimālia, became governor of Maui in 1812. For a time he was cogovernor with Kamehameha's young son, Kekūāiwa Kamehameha.[50] The governorship of the islands (kia 'āina) was a relatively new level in the hierarchy of chiefs, first established by Kahekili II of Maui when he was also paramount over Lāna'i, Moloka'i, and O'ahu. Kia 'āina such as Kalanikūpule were essentially viceroys for the king. The seat of the Maui governor was at Lahaina.

After returning to Hawai'i, Kamehameha lived out his remaining years. His third child with Keōpūolani, Kauikeaouli, was born in Keauhou, North Kona, on 17 March 1814. A fourth child, a daughter named Nāhi'ena'ena, was born in 1815. The three sacred children of Keōpūolani and Kamehameha I were to conclude the era of divine rulers of the Hawaiian Islands. They had in their blood the mana of the gods, and they were the children of mo'o Kihawahine herself.

By now Kihawahine had become a symbol of the momentous changes Hawaiian society faced with the introduction of foreign religion, concepts of private property and money, and the specter of devastating epidemics. Around 1815, at the death of Kamehameha I's son Kekūāiwa Kamehameha, who helped rule Maui with Kahekilike'eaumoku, the mo'o Mokuhinia was reportedly seen at Kalepolepo at Kīhei.[51] This was also the time that the sacred mother of Keōpūolani, Keku'iapoiwa Liliha, died.[52]

Ka-lani-kau-i-ke-aouli (The Exhalted One Placed in the Dark Cloud) Kīwalaʻō (after his grandfather) Ke-aweawe-ʻula (The Red Trail [of the gods]) was given to the *kahuna* (priest) Kaikioʻewa to be raised. Until the age of five he was guarded by Kaikioʻewa at ʻOʻoma, Kekaha, in North Kona, Hawaiʻi. His companions were Keaweamahi, Kahouokalani, and Koakanu. In addition to being raised in a traditional manner as a divine Hawaiian *aliʻi,* he also played with a toy boat rigged as a Western warship. It had a genuine miniature cannon that the future king used to fill with real powder.[53] Keōpūolani was exceptionally close to her children and did not wish them to be separated from her, as was the custom of *hānai.* Happily, she kept Princess Nāhiʻenaʻena with her throughout.

E oni wale no ʻoukou i kuʻu pono ʻaʻole e pau—"Endless is the good that I have given you to enjoy." With those words, King Kamehameha I expired in Kailua-Kona, Hawaiʻi, on 14 May 1819. He had entrusted the hiding of his bones to his closest friend, Hoapili. The bones of fallen chiefs, packed with *mana,* were especially coveted by enemies to defile them or to make magical fishhooks, *kahili* handles, or arrowheads from them. When Kamehameha's sennit-wrapped remains (*kāʻai*) were ready, Hoapili and Keōpūolani rowed across the lake at Kaloko and placed them in a secret cave. It was said that the hiding place also contained the bones of the sacred Kalola Pupuka and King Kahekili II.[54] They have never been found.

Chapter 3
Queen Keōpūolani Returns Home

A momentous event associated with the death of Kamehameha I was the decision by the new king, Liholiho Kamehameha II, not to reestablish the *kapu* system, thus ending the power of the priests and most of the traditional state religion of Hawai'i. Ironically, the end of the system coincided closely with the move of the royal court back to Lahaina and the sacred island of Moku'ula.

The court marked the death of Kamehameha I by the traditional lifting of all *kapu,* personal as well as those of food. When his son was installed as king by Queen Regent Ka'ahumanu, however, the *kapu* were not reestablished. Instead, the queens dowager Ka'ahumanu, Kaheiheimālia, and Keōpūolani convinced Liholiho to keep free eating (*'ainoa*) a permanent arrangement. Kamakau recalls the event:

> Liholiho returned by canoe to Kailua, and the next day Ka-'ahu-manu proclaimed him king. Ke-opu-o-lani then looked at the young chief and put her hand to her mouth as a sign for free eating. This was a strange thing for a tabu chiefess to do, one for whom these tabus were made and who had the benefit of them. How could those to whom the tabu rank did not belong object after that? In the afternoon she ate with Kau-i-ke-aouli, and it was through her influence alone that the eating tabu was freed.[55]

For a brief time the *kapu* was reestablished by Liholiho, but then he proclaimed *'ainoa* throughout the kingdom. The state religion that had kept the divine *ali'i* apart from the commoners through the *kapu* system overtly came to a halt. In 1820 puritan missionaries from Boston began to arrive, sent from the American Board of Commissioners for Foreign Missions, which was an interdenominational congregation of Presbyterians and Congregationalists.[56] They were impressed by the acts of the young king: "The eldest son of the Conqueror of Ha-wai-i had ascended the throne, and the very opening of his reign had been marked by a measure which is without a parallel in the history of the world. A pagan king, unbidden and uninstructed, had in a day cast off all the gods of his people; and, by a single stroke of boldness, overthrown a superstition, which, for ages, had held a degraded race in the bondage of fear."[57] Indeed, the fires went out on the platforms of temples throughout the archipelago, and great *ki'i* images were tossed into the sea.

New Homes, New Influence

Kauikeaouli and sister Nāhi'ena'ena accompanied their brother Liholiho on an 1820 trip to Maui. The little prince and princess established residences in Lahaina; the young king continued on to Honolulu. On O'ahu, Kamehameha II constructed a residence at Pākākā *heiau*, adjacent to the former houses of his father. The *ali'i* were now advising the king to select a permanent address. Perhaps referring to the instability and local tyranny of the traditional system, Kalanimoku pointed out "the evils which had resulted from the king's not being fixed in any particular place."[58] In actuality, it was the development of a monetized economy and foreign trade that made a central residence convenient in the extraction of tribute and taxation.

Kauikeaouli stayed in Lahaina with his *kahu* Kaikio'ewa. The chief Kalau'alu became the little prince's personal attendant. A good description of Lahaina at the time was penned by French Captain Louis Claude Desaules de Freycinet, who visited the Lahaina encampment at Keawaiki in August 1819, soon after the death of Kamehameha on Hawai'i:

> We immediately landed, M. Lamarche and myself, with a view to visiting the watering place and to select an appropriate location for setting up our instruments. Kiaimoukou [Ke'eaumoku] went with us and, upon my request, was kind enough to tabou a platform in the neighborhood of a morai [heiau] and of a red brick house, which was convenient for our future operations. These tabou formalities assured us that our observations would not be overrun by curious visitors. Not far away, the watering place was found to be most convenient.... Standing right next to the landing point [the red brick house], it was an excellent guide for the vessels. It is said that originally Tamehameha had intended this to be a storehouse, but the construction was so defective that it began to sag in plain view when it was hardly completed. To the south was the habitation of the priests and next to it a morai constructed on a pile of dry rocks and forming a sort of dike on the beach. A little farther up in the interior one

comes across hand-dug reservoirs used for taro culture. They stretch along the coast for quite some distance and are fed by the streams brought there through artificial canals. The houses, instead of being grouped next to each other, are dispersed over a rather wide terrain that, in striking contrast to the surroundings of the towns described earlier, presents an appearance of freshness and fertility all over.[59]

Queen Keōpūolani soon took up residence in Lahaina herself. She had been immediately attracted to the Christian missionaries and would become the paramount symbol of two conflicting worlds. She and her daughter were the last female *ali'i* whose *mana* was that of the old *akua* themselves, and Keōpūolani would become the "first fruit" of the Christian mission, a woman who overthrew the very privileges of status that made her the highest personage in the land. In 1823 she informed the mission at Kona of her intention to retire to her home in Lahaina, and she wished some of the missionaries to accompany her. Her husband Ulumaheiheihoapili had just been appointed governor of Maui. But she was, in fact, dying.

C. S. Stewart and William Richards were the American preachers chosen by the mission for residence in Lahaina. Liholiho provided his ship, *Cleopatra's Barge,* for the journey to Maui. Stewart remarked how lovingly the king saw his mother to the ship, which set sail from O'ahu with about 200 chiefs and courtiers on 30 May 1823. The great counselor Kalanimoku led the party escorting the queen dowager to Lahaina.

Compared to the dry, dusty streets of Honolulu, the peaceful, verdant gardens of Lahaina proved a stunning contrast: "The thick shade of the bread-fruit trees which surround [their hosts'] cottages—the rustling of the breeze through the bananas and sugar-cane—the murmurs of the mountain streams encircling the yard—and the coolness and verdure of every spot around us—seemed … like the delights of an Eden." After the initial impression of Lahaina, however, Stewart began to see flaws in his paradise: "There is no uniformity or neatness to be seen, and almost every thing seems to be growing in the wildness of nature.… All these flourish exuberantly from the richness of the soil alone, with but little attention or labour from the hand of man."[60]

Almost immediately the missionaries began to proselytize the Native Hawaiians, about 2,500 of whom lived in Lahaina. The chiefs and the court were instructed in reading, writing, and religion. Hoapili resided with Keōpūolani.[61] The queen's daughter, Nāhi'ena'ena, maintained her own household at Lahaina, most likely at Moku'ula. Keōpūolani's son Kauikeaouli maintained his household at Halaka'a in Lahaina under the care of Kaikio'ewa, Kahouokalani, and Kapololu.[62] The queen was generous in providing the new mission with produce, land, and help of every kind. Lahaina was in full flower.

Like Stewart, French seaman Jacques Arago noted the renaissance of Lahaina productivity, recalling the causeways being built across the fishponds of Kaluaʻehu. In 1823 he wrote:

> The environs of Lahaina are like a garden. It would be difficult to find a soil more fertile, or a people who can turn it to greater advantage; little pathways sufficiently raised, and kept in excellent condition, serve as communications between the different estates. These are frequently divided by trenches, through which a fresh and limpid stream flows tranquilly, giving life to the plantations, the sole riches of the country. Hollow squares, of the depth of two, three, and sometimes four feet, nourish various sorts of vegetables and plants; amongst which we distinguish the Caribee-cabbage, named here *taro;* double rows of banana, bread-fruit, cocoa-nut, *palma-christi,* and the paper-mulberry trees, intercept the rays of the sun, and allow you to walk at mid-day.... beyond this all is dry and barren; everything recalls the image of desolation.[63]

Much of Lahaina seems to have remained in this state until sugar plantations drastically changed the land use in the area near the end of the nineteenth century.

In June 1823, King Kamehameha II paid a visit to his mother at Lahaina. Keōpūolani tried in vain to get her son to stop his renowned revelries, his drinking and his dalliances. On 5 July, Kamehameha II, with his chiefs and wives, set sail for Molokaʻi.

Death of the Great Queen

One by one the chiefs of the islands arrived to pay their respects to ailing Keōpūolani in Lahaina. On her deathbed she was attended by Hoapili, Kamehameha II and Queen Kamāmalu, Prince Kauikeaouli, Princess Nāhiʻenaʻena, King Kaumualiʻi of Kauaʻi, Queen Kaʻahumanu, Prime Minister Kalanimoku, and Keōpūolani's protestant ministers, Stewart and Bingham. On 16 September 1823, the queen was baptized a Christian, then passed away. The mission had been particularly anxious that the occasion of her death would spark a riot of debauchery and violence, which had been traditional with the demise of a high chief—and Keōpūolani was the highest in the land.

Keōpūolani's funeral was a mixture of traditional and Christian rites—the first of its kind in Hawaiʻi. She had left explicit instructions that traditional rites, including acts of self-mortification, were not to be held: "I do not wish the customs of Hawaii to be observed when I die. Put me in a coffin, and bury me in the earth in a Christian manner." Stewart, who was actually at the funeral, noted that no "pagan" rites were followed: "We need not entertain any apprehension whatever, that Keopuolani had long before forbidden every heathen practice at her death;

and that the people had received the strictest orders against all their former [funeral] customs, except *wailing.*"[64]

The traditional method of burial of an *ali'i nui* often included stripping the bones of their flesh and burial of the sennit-wrapped bones (*kā'ai*) in a secret place (*huna kele*). Some chiefs were salted to preserve the corpse (called *i'a loa,* "long fish").[65] To show respect for the dead, mourners often had a tooth knocked out or their hair cropped. According to the wishes of Keōpūolani, however, the populace was only allowed to wail (Figure 7).

Stewart's account of the entombment continues:[66] "She was, at two o'clock to-day, deposited in a substantial mud-and-stone house, lately built by the princess. This is the first Christian funeral of a high chief that has ever taken place in the islands.... How different the rites of her sepulture from those of her fathers!" It seems that the tomb was built in anticipation of Keōpūolani's death. A few days later, on 24 September 1823, Stewart noted:

> The whole district, men, women, and children, to the number of some thousands, have been daily engaged this week in carrying stones from the old *heiau* [Wailehua *heiau* at Mākila], or idolatrous temple, on the south point, to the place where Keopuolani is buried, to build a wall and monument around the house in which she is deposited: headed and assisted by their chiefs, male and female, of every rank, they have engaged

Figure 7. Lamentations for Keōpūolani. Hoapili stands immediately in front of the sacred Prince Kauikeaouli and Princess Nāhi'ena'ena, who are being carried on the shoulders of their guardians. Engraving by Barber after a drawing by the missionary William Ellis (in *Memoir of Keopuolani,* 1825, Crocker & Brewster, Boston).

in the work with much spirit, and pass and repass our door in troops of a hundred and more at a time, singing their rude songs with as much merriment, as with bitterness last week they seemed to wail.... They are all followed by their *kahiles;* and I have smiled more than once to see a queen or royal princess carrying a large stone, while a stout man, behind her, had borne nothing but a light feathered staff, to proclaim the dignity of his mistress.

To recall, Wailehua had been built by her royal Maui ancestor, King Kamehamehanui. Bingham, who became the *kahuna nui* of the new faith, stated: "The relatives and friends of the deceased brought stones from the ruins of an old neighboring heathen temple, and laying them up into a wall, enclosed the tomb where they had deposited their friend."[67]

The funeral of this "first fruit" of the mission was reported back home in Boston: "Her remains were deposited in a very tight stone and mud house. Around the house was built a stone wall from 6 to 12 feet thick, and from 4 to 10 feet high. This was a great work. The stones were all carried by hand, a distance of about a mile, and then laid in clay."[68]

Richards's account placed special emphasis on the uniqueness of the new, Western-style funeral:[69] "All in the procession, amounting to about four hundred, were dressed in European style, except a few who fell in the rear after the procession first moved. The path was thronged on every side, by thousands of the people, who had never witnessed any thing of the kind before." Richards's letters follow Stewart's recollection of the event: "Minute guns were fired from the ships in the roads, and the bell continued tolling until the corpse was deposited in the place prepared for it, which was a new house built of stone and cemented with mud, designed as a tomb for the chiefs."

During the extended period of mourning, Native Hawaiians created a large encampment around the tomb: "The body was deposited in the place appointed for it. The relatives and high chiefs encamped immediately around the house, and are now busily engaged in erecting temporary booths; designing to live near the body for some time to come."[70] Regarding this activity, Richards noted:

> Temporary dwellings were immediately erected by the chiefs around the house where she was laid, and in them they resided for several weeks, as a testimony of their affection for the deceased. They spent much of their time in conversing about their departed chief, and the charges she had given them during her last sickness. Whenever any persons arrived from any part of the islands, they went and seated themselves beside her tomb, and there indulged in grief and lamentation.[71]

The *maka'āinana*, as well as the *ali'i*, were making a pilgrimage locus of the site of Keōpūolani's entombment in stone, an action that seems partially traditional and partially innovative. This activity would set a precedent for Kauikeaouli's creation of a similar tomb on Moku'ula twelve years later. From this nucleus, the capital of the Kingdom of the Hawaiian Islands would be reestablished at Lahaina. Hawaiian historian Thomas Thrum suggested that 1824 was the year it was made official.[72]

By far the most difficult issue in the analysis of Moku'ula is the status of the tomb of Keōpūolani. Traditionalists such as Inez Ashdown claim that the queen mother was originally buried at Moku'ula, secreted away, her bones perhaps hidden in a cave in the calm of the lake, in the manner of the hiding of Kamehameha I's remains (also under the supervision of Hoapili). But primary missionary accounts, as well as the recollection of others who visited her tomb in later years, do not place her initial sepulcher on Moku'ula, but nearer the beach and to the north in the area known as the enclosure (*pā*) Halekamani in adjacent Pākalā.

"Ke-opu-o-lani died September 16, 1823, at Kaluaokiha [the pit of Kiha] in Lahaina in her fifty-fifth year"[73]: From these succinct words of Kamakau, it cannot be demonstrated that the great chiefess expired at Moku'ula. After she became a Christian, however, it seems unlikely that Keōpūolani would have resided at Moku'ula. She was not ignorant of the significance of the sacred place to traditional Hawaiian religious practices and beliefs. Now, her lofty *kapu* had no significance for her, nor would a moated island palace separating her from her beloved missionaries suffice. From the accounts of Stewart, the queen died at her residence on the beach at the Halekamani area.[74] This region, being adjacent to Loko o Mokuhinia to the north, may have also been part of the place referred to as Kalua o Kiha within the larger Kalua'ehu. The great stone and clay wall most likely enclosed the entire estate of Halekamani, forming a seawall on one side. Portions of this wall still exist.

The large walled enclosure created a space for residential buildings for chiefs in addition to the tomb of stone and rock: "within the yard are erected two houses, in which the chiefs live. Some of them will probably spend their lives there. Krimokoo [Kalanimoku] said to the king 'I have heretofore designed living at Woahoo [O'ahu], but in consequence of my great love for Keopuolani, let me sit down here by her side, until we be both dead together.'"[75]

From one source, the site of the tomb is contained within the old fort of Lahaina: "More towards the town on the sea beach, is a mud battery in bad repair, mounted with five cannon, in the same, neglected state. Within its walls is a small mud hut, whitewashed outside, where had been buried lately one of Tamahamaah's queens. Near this fort, the missionaries have a small thatched chapel, with dwelling houses and garden grounds."[76] This "fort" is the royal enclosure along the beach, which includes Halekamani. It was fortified by the placement of stones from Wailehua *heiau*. In fact, the location of the tomb next to or within the fortifications built to protect the port and the royal residences practically precludes the first tomb being at Mokuʻula, which is inland of the beach.

Macrae's description of this old fort is substantiated by Richard Bloxam: "We found here a mud-built fort containing four guns and surrounding a closed shed, or mausoleum, in which were buried the remains of the mother of the late king [Liholiho]."[77]

In his book on Keōpūolani, Mitsuo Uyehara, augmented the Duperrey map of 1823 [1819], placing her tomb in the enclosure of Nāhiʻenaʻena's house, Pā Halekamani. He also superimposed Loko o Mokuhinia upon the Duperrey map, the original of which omitted the pond.[78]

The idea of a Western-style mausoleum was an innovation to Native Hawaiians in the early nineteenth century. And Keōpūolani's later years were lived any way but according to tradition: she eased the *kapu* surrounding her own self and banned human sacrifice for infractions; she encouraged Liholiho to free the eating prohibitions; Keōpūolani and Kaʻahumanu had the young king overthrow the gods. The royal women adopted the ways and religion of the *haole* and their new sources of *mana*. One doubts that Keōpūolani herself would have entertained continued association with her "dark pagan" past through residence or entombment at the *kapu* site appropriate to her as the child of Kihawahine—Mokuʻula.

Pā Halekamani

After the death of Kamehameha I, the *kuhina nui* Kaʻahumanu married Kaumualiʻi, the last king of an independent Kauaʻi, and his son. They lived with her at Nīhoa in Honolulu, near Kamehameha II's palace at Pākākā. Kamakau suggests that the Kauaʻi king made a request that his body be not removed to Kauaʻi but taken to Lahaina and buried at the feet of the chiefess Keōpūolani. He died in May 1824 and was reported to have been interred at the entrance of Keōpūolani's tomb at Kalua o Kiha.[79]

This probably should not be taken too literally. The Reverend William Ellis attended the funeral of the last king of Kauaʻi and wrote:

> I accompanied the chiefs with the corpse to Maui on the 28th; and on the 30th, which was the sabbath, his interment took place at Lahaina, in a style somewhat similar though less imposing, than that in which Keopuolani's remains had been conveyed to the tomb. Taumuarii [Kaumualiʻi] and Keopuolani agreed, prior to her decease, that directions should be given, to have their bodies deposited side by side together in the grave, they might rise together in the morning of the resurrection. This was

complied with, and the body of Taumuarii was placed by the side of his late departed friend.[80]

Considering that the devout Kaumualiʻi and Keōpūolani tended to follow the advice of missionaries in all matters of Christian ritual, most likely Ellis's account is the more accurate. Conceivably, Kaumualiʻi was buried in a coffin placed next to that of Keōpūolani, at the tomb at Pā Halekamani. The king's countrymen on Kauaʻi, unlike those who had restrained their behavior during the wake of Keōpūolani, broke into traditional riotous behavior during the mourning period, a prelude to the Kauaʻi rebellion that was soon to follow.[81]

Immediately after the death of his mother, Liholiho, King Kamehameha II, announced from Kalua o Kiha his impending visit to England. He appointed his younger brother Kauikeaouli to serve in his stead. The royal couple set off for England in November 1823 in a whaling ship. They were accompanied by Boki, James Young Kānehoa, Liliha, Kekūanāoʻa, and several other chiefs. Kānehoa, who carried letters of introduction to the Court of St. James, missed his ship when in port in Rio de Janeiro, and thus the Hawaiian king and queen encountered delayed arrangements upon their arrival in England. As a consequence, they never were to meet King George IV. While waiting for the credentials to be straightened out, King Kamehameha II and Queen Kamāmalu contracted measles and quickly succumbed.[82]

King Kamehameha II and Queen Kamāmalu died in London in July 1824. In May of the following year, their bodies were returned to the Hawaiian kingdom on the H.M.S. *Blonde*. The ship anchored offshore at Lahaina. With the dreadful news, Kauikeaouli, 11 years old, was proclaimed King Kamehameha III. According to Cummins Speakman's history of Maui, "the bodies of the King Liholiho and Queen Kamāmalu were brought ashore and carried to the small island, a tabu spot sacred to the chiefs, where they remained lying in state until the *Blonde* was made ready for the trip to Honolulu. The chiefs went aboard for the sad journey to Honolulu, accompanied by Hoapili, Nāhiʻenaʻena, and Kauikeaouli, the Prince, now to become King Kamehameha the Third."[83]

Thus, it appears that they were brought over to Mokuʻula. Speakman does not specify his sources, however, and the only primary, eyewitness account contradicts him. According to Richards, Chief Boki took a launch from the *Blonde* to the shore, where he was met by Hoapili. While the populace broke into mournful wailing, the bodies, in their heavy, nested coffins, apparently stayed aboard the ship—it was becalmed several miles offshore. Later that day the *Blonde* managed to anchor closer in, just off the Lahaina reef. In the late afternoon of the next day, the ship was joined by the new king and Princess Nāhiʻenaʻena for the trip to Oʻahu. The bodies were removed from the ship at Māmala in Honolulu (Pākākā Point wharf) with great pomp and were buried in a house at Kalanimoku's resi-

Figure 8. Edward Finden's engraving based on Robert Dampier's portrait of King Kamehameha III, 1825. Hawaii State Archives.

dence. According to these sources, Kamehameha II and Queen Kamāmalu were never buried in Lahaina, although it is possible that they spent the night lying in state at Halekamani.[84]

With the death of his brother, young Kauikeaouli mounted the throne as King Kamehameha III (Figure 8). During the mid-1820s, while his sister Nāhiʻenaʻena stayed with her stepfather Hoapili and his new wife Kaheiheimālia[85] on Maui, the young king and his court returned to Honolulu. A new region of residence for the court was established at Pohukaina, near the houses and church of the American Mission. This was the decision of the queen regent and *kuhina nui* Kaʻahumanu, who wished to be close to the center of foreign trade and the mission. When the king was old enough, he would rectify the move to Oʻahu and return to Lahaina.

The next documented burial of a Maui *aliʻi nui* at Lahaina was that of Kahakuhaʻakoi Wahine Piʻo, sister of chiefs Kalanimoku and Boki, wife of Kahoʻanoku Kīnaʻu (son of Kamehameha I), and mother of Kekauʻōnohi. She died in an epidemic of bronchitis while in residence at Mokuʻula. This reference[86] is the earliest documentation of residence on the sacred island. For two years after the death of Kahekilikeʻeaumoku in 1824, Wahine Piʻo had been governor of Maui. Her funeral was briefly described by missionaries: "The funeral of Wahine Pio was attended on Monday the 22nd and her remains deposited in the tomb of Keopuolani."[87] Her death was followed soon by that of Liliha's mother, Kaʻilikauoha, daughter of Maui King Kahekili II by Kauwahine.[88] Kaʻilikauoha had been the first wife of Hoapili. Liliha was the wife of Governor Boki of Oʻahu:

When I awoke in the morning, I found a man waiting at the door in the greatest agony having his hands almost consumed by fire. The above mentioned woman (Kailikauoha—"former wife of Hoapili and the mother of Mrs. Poki") died on the 5th and yesterday her remains were deposited in the tomb of Keopuolani. As is the custom of the chiefs they all went into the tomb, or house of deposit that they might sleep beside their departed chief. The house was divided into rooms by curtains which hung around in great abundance. At midnight when the chiefs were all asleep, with the door open, a man without, perceived the curtains to be all in a flame. He instantly awoke the chiefs & with considerable presence of mind seized the curtains, rolled them up and carried them out of the house. As the house was grass, it must in one moment have caught the fire.[89]

By all other accounts, the tomb was stone, not grass. It may have been confused with the *hale pili,* or thatched huts, which could have been constructed by the *ali'i* in the vicinity of the tomb.

Two other interments are noted for the old Lahaina mausoleum of Halekamani in the late 1820s. The compound and even the tomb itself were later used for residences. In a reference to the burial of the chiefess Kiliwehi, "the funeral took place two days after her death and her remains were deposited beside the remains of our former patroness, Keopuolani." Kiliwehi's brother Chief Kaiko'okalani seems to have died around that time as well: "[Captain Clasby] brought notice from Lahaina that Kaiko, a high chief there, died during his stay and was reposited in the house erected for the cemetery of the chiefs; which enclosed the remains of Keopuolani and Taumuarii [Kaumuali'i]." Kaiko'okalani and Kiliwehi were children of Kamehameha I by Peleuli Kamehameha and thus would have been of very high rank.[90]

The record is subsequently almost completely silent on burials at Pā Halekamani. During this time, however, Princess Nāhi'ena'ena established or embelished her household there. In referring to the stone and mortar style of building that was becoming fashionable in Lahaina, Stewart suggests that in 1829 "one [stone building] not entirely completed belongs to the princess."[91] Since there are no other accounts of stone buildings in Lahaina belonging to Nāhi'ena'ena, the reference may not refer to her house at Halekamani. By all accounts, Nāhi'ena'ena's house at Halekamani was a *hale pili.* One such account is by Gorham Gilman, a future tenant (1851–61): "This was one of the finest straw houses in the village, erected in a plot of ground partly reclining from the beach with sea walls in front and planted with kou trees. The house was some thirty by forty feet in dimensions. The interior was lined by dry banana stalks, and had hard earth floors cov-

Figure 9. The finely thatched Halekamani, built for Princess Nāhiʻenaʻena. Occupied ca. 1823–61. Bishop Museum CP 29536.

ered with fine mats."[92] Figure 9 is a watercolor of the glazed-window, thatched Halekamani when it was occupied by Gilman.

According to the plan view of Pā Halekamani in the Van Dyke collection[93] and S. E. Bishop's survey of Lahaina (1884), the tomb of Halekamani was directly south of Nāhiʻenaʻena's house. This may be the small building on the extreme right of the watercolor. It seems that Stewart's 1829 comment on Nāhiʻenaʻena's stone house being built at another location was a reference to construction on the sacred island of Mokuʻula.

The enclosed houselot of Halekamani had been given to Kamehameha III and Nāhiʻenaʻena by Keōpūolani, according to the king's Mahele claim of 1848. It was the sacred queen mother's lands, probably part of the original settlement of Kamehameha I during 1802. Provisions had been made for Mikahela Kekauʻōnohi to *mālama* (keep in trust) this royal compound after her cousin Nāhiʻenaʻena's death in 1836 (LCA 10806), although the claim was later contested by Kekauʻōnohi's husband, who wanted the property for himself. According to the king's claim, Halekamani was occupied anciently by Keōpūolani, who died and was buried there. Kalanimoku, who was a relative of the king's mother, had placed the enclosure in charge of Kekauʻōnohi as a guardian of the tomb.[94]

Traditional Religion and Christianity in the Late 1820s

The ancient Hawaiian religious system did not disappear with the rather histrionic banquet of the chiefesses and Liholiho staged soon after the death of Kamehameha I. Evidence of a continuation of the archaic religion began in the late 1820s, and it sheds light on the status of the royal tomb of the Maui *aliʻi* in Lahaina and the mindset of young King Kamehameha III.

Kaʻahumanu, the powerful regent, had certainly utilized the new *kapu* of the Protestant mission to maintain and enhance her novel position as *kuhina nui* and virtual ruler of the kingdom. The formal split between secular and sacred responsibilities of kingship was not a innovative introduction by the missionaries, however. A dyarchy of kingship roles existed traditionally in Hawai'i, consisting of an "active" ruler of inferior rank and a "passive" one of superior rank—the conqueror on the path of Kū and the peaceful leader whose actions reflect the ideals of Lono.[95] A reconstructed dyarchy of rule was to continue well into the nineteenth century in Hawai'i. Three successive *kuhina nui,* the Maui *ali'i wahine* Ka'ahumanu, Kīna'u, and Kekāuluohi, would play the fierce god Kū, while Kauikeaouli acted the part of gentle, nurturing Lono—the pattern was ancient and must have been remembered by the rulers of the early unified kingdom.

Kīwala'ō, the sacred son of Kalani'ōpu'u and Kalola of Maui and father of Keōpūolani, had been ritually superior to his cousin Kamehameha, the active usurper on the path of Kū. The fortunes of the latter are well known. In the following generation, his son Liholiho was given the responsibilities of maintaining Kamehameha I's *akua* deities and the ritual life of the kingdom—Liholiho was a grandson of the legitimate Kīwala'ō and the son of *kapu* chiefess Keōpūolani. Through her and her child by Kamehameha, a synthesis of the Maui and senior Hawai'i royal lines was accomplished—a repeating, valuable political structure known in structural history as a system of the *longue durée.* The metaphor of legitimating an usurper through the production of an heir of higher rank was not discarded in the overthrow of the *kapu* system in 1819.

The reproduction of the structure of the Kū/Lono opposition and synthesis was seriously impaired, however, with the arrival of Cook in 1778. Contact with the West began a process "that ultimately brought about the transcendence of that opposition by transcending war and human sacrifice once and for all."[96] After the abolition of the *kapu* system at the death of Kamehameha I, the power in the kingdom was first secularized (the *kapu* freed), then seized by Ka'ahumanu (the new *kapu* bound). Traditional legitimacy, based in sacred right, was the now-empty Lono mantle inherited by Liholiho and Kauikeaouli. This emptiness was to haunt Kauikeaouli for the rest of his life.

In a very real sense, Ka'ahumanu was the usurper, utilizing the powers of the new god Jehovah to conquer and reestablish the *kapu.* Her most famous edicts, mostly dealing with propriety, were in fact nothing more than New England blue laws.[97] No doubt Ka'ahumanu and her Christian supporters were sensitive to the phenomenon of the tomb of Keōpūolani and its cultist potential for revivalists. This is probably the main reason that the original Christian tomb of the Maui *ali'i* was *not* established on Moku'ula. To have placed the *kapu* chiefess in the grotto of Kihawahine, to some the *piko* of Hawaiian cosmology, would have tempted those very forces Ka'ahumanu and the missionaries had been fighting against. The site may have become a place of pilgrimage for Native Hawaiians.

Ka'ahumanu's attitude toward traditional *ali'i* mortuary practices is illuminated by Bingham. He recalls her blasphemous actions toward the holy burial grounds on the island of Hawai'i. In 1828–29, upon the suspicion that Hawaiians had been deifying the bones of the Kamehameha ancestors *('unihipili),* the queen regent apparently had the sennit-wrapped bones of Līloa, Lonoikamakahiki, and other chiefs removed from the *heiau* in Waipi'o Valley. She also relocated the mortuary contents of Hale o Keawe at Hōnaunau in Kona:

> The regent visited the place not to mingle her adorations with her early contemporaries and predecessors to the relics of departed mortals, but for the purpose of removing the bones of twenty-four deified kings and princes of the Hawaiian race, and consigning them to oblivion.... in company with Mr. Ruggles and Kapiolani, she went to the sacred deposit, in a cave in the precipice at the head of Kealakekua Bay. In doing this she found an expensive article of foreign manufacture, comparatively new, placed near the bones of the father of Kekauluohi [Kaleimamahū], and which appeared to have been presented as an offering since the date of the prohibition of the worship of idols.[98]

According to Kamakau, "She ... had the chiefs' bones burned, the house broken down, and the hidden bones of the chiefs brought out and shown publicly." The bones of generations of chiefs down to Kalani'ōpu'u and Kīwala'ō were then hidden in a cave at Ka'awaloa, and unknown remains burned. In fact, many of the bones were moved several times, acts that no doubt were akin to the traditional revengeful deeds of a conqueror. It was an action that "embittered Boki further against her." Given her attitude, it seems unlikely the powerful regent would have encouraged the populace of Lahaina in their attempt to revive traditional veneration toward *ali'i* remains deposited in that royal community.[99]

Ka'ahumanu probably did have cause for concern in Lahaina, too. All the old ways had not been buried with Keōpūolani, and it was also clear that the *maka'āinana* were at times reluctant to follow the ways of the new religion, even at one of its principal loci: "Notwithstanding all the charges which [Keōpūolani] gave, and all the light which has been communicated by the missionaries, there are many superstitions prevailing respecting her. Some of the people assert, and appear to believe, that she had not gone to heaven, saying that her soul had been seen by many of the people living on her land."[100] Could this refer to the sightings of the *mo'o* Kihawahine in the years following Keōpūolani's death?

As Ka'ahumanu's grip weakened with old age, the kingdom experienced increasingly frequent episodes of revival of the ancient rites. The anti-Christian faction among the *ali'i* was strong and included competent and popular figures such as Boki, Liliha, Pākī, Kauikeaouli, and his courtiers. The establishment of the royal tomb and residence at Moku'ula, the *noho* of Kihawahine and her descendants, became possible during this period of Native Hawaiian revitalization.

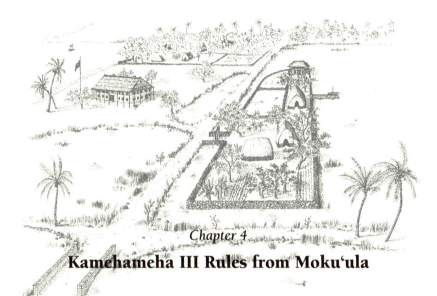

Chapter 4
Kamehameha III Rules from Moku'ula

Like the dualism in the traditional path of the usurper and the nurturer, the lives of Kamehameha III and his sister Nāhi'ena'ena's were characterized by powerful internal contradictions. Which path was *pono* (righteous)? The heavenly trail of the ancestors or the powerful new religion of the black-robed missionaries from America? It can be seen now that the struggle only began in 1819. Neither the entire body of *ali'i* nor the *maka'āinana* were ready to abandon their cultural traditions completely in the instant that the permanent *'ainoa* was proclaimed.

Students of Hawaiian history have been provided by Marjorie Sinclair with a riveting account of the psychological conflicts of Nāhi'ena'ena (Figure 10), torn between her exalted traditional position as the *akua* princess with the "*kapu* of raging fire" and the *mana* of Kihawahine, and her mother's request that she be raised to become a docile, God-fearing housewife in the style of the missionaries.[101] A similar psychological conflict afflicted her brother Kauikeaouli, who not only held the same rank as a *nī'aupi'o* chief but had the added tension of being the sovereign of a rapidly changing kingdom. He had watched as powerful female regents, the Christian Ka'ahumanu and her successor Kīna'u, took many of the prerogatives of supreme authority away from the king, using the *mana* of their new *akua* to fortify their own positions.

During the early post-Kamehameha I years of the Hawaiian kingdom, this dualism was manifest in a socio-religious parallelism at the Loko o Mokuhinia region of Lahaina, a parallelism that developed in response to Western culture contact and the operation of the dynamics of change. In Lahaina, the houses of the Calvinist missionaries, their Waine'e Church, the households of the Christian Hoapili, the court and retainers (*mā*) of Ka'ahumanu, and the port community itself, with its worldly tradesmen, sailors, and shops, represented the new power.

Figure 10. Princess Nāhiʻenaʻena in 1826 with feather cape and *kahili.* Engraving by Edwin Finden after an oil by Robert Dampier. Hawaii State Archives.

This was the new *mana,* based on the word of the Western God, the *haole* printed word, cash, and the attendant material culture reflective of a global economy. The physical center of these changing political, economic, and religious landscapes—surrounded as it was by the church, the modern stone houses of Christian chiefs, and the new, Hale Piula palace—was the ancient Kaluaʻehu and Loko o Mokuhinia. The center within, Mokuʻula, represented the power of tradition—a traditional source of *mana* and legitimacy under attack by the forces of foreign-imposed change.

In the 1830s, Kauikeaouli transformed Nāhiʻenaʻena's modest residence at Mokuʻula into a new mausoleum for the untimely demise of his sister. Subsequently he added the bodies of his mother Keōpūolani and other chiefs brought over from the tomb at nearby Halekamani. For the next eight years, Mokuʻula would be Kauikeaouli's home—a refuge away from the control of Kaʻahumanu's successor, Kīnaʻu, and her bluff husband on Oʻahu. Mokuʻula was the one place his *kapu* held, under the protection, it would seem, of his ancestress Kihawahine. Mokuʻula, soon to again become the cultural and spiritual *piko* of the Hawaiian people, was the last resort of the traditional Hawaiian monarchy and the ancestral home of its last divine king.

Breaking the New Kapu

The return of the capital to Maui, like most major events, was built upon a set of events and circumstances that were both unrelated and unanticipated. Young King Kamehameha III, now in his early teens, had been staying with his *kahu* Kahalaiʻa in Honolulu until the priest's death in 1826 (Figure 11). Then Kauikeaouli's household retreated to the mountains of Waikalua and Mokuleʻia on Oʻahu to cut sandalwood, in that frantic era when cash-hungry Hawaiian nobility stripped the forests of their land to harvest the precious wood. It was during this time that Governor Boki commandeered his men to build a splendid new house for the king on Beretania Street in Honolulu. It was called Kahaleʻuluhe, the Fern House, for its special fern thatching. The royal cousins were close: Kauikeaouli himself helped Boki's men build the extensive rock wall around the Boki estate at Punahou (which is still standing). Both Boki and Kauikeaouli had difficult dealings with Kaʻahumanu, and both shared their love for the beautiful Liliha, only daughter of Hoapili.[102]

In 1828 the king and his court visited Lahaina for the first time since he had left as the new king in 1825. There he was reunited with his stepfather Hoapili, cousin Kekauʻōnohi, sister Nāhiʻenaʻena, and other great *aliʻi* of Maui. He returned briefly in 1829 to fetch Nāhiʻenaʻena and the Maui chiefs to attend the dedication of Kawai-a-Haʻo Church at Pohukaina in Honolulu. Also that year, Governor Boki sailed away to the New Hebrides aboard the king's ship *Kamehameha* to harvest sandalwood reputedly growing there in great abundance. Boki had amassed great debts that Kaʻahumanu would not forgive. Boki was never seen again.[103]

Figure 11. King Kamehameha III as a young man. Hawaii State Archives.

The *kapu* system had not been overthrown in 1819. Rather, it was replaced by a series of foreign prohibitions through Kaʻahumanu and her followers.[104] Individual decorum was now regulated by Calvinist virtue: alcohol was *kapu;* sibling marriage among the *aliʻi* was now sinfully incestuous; monogamy rather than plural marriages (*punalua*) was enforced; guiltless sexual pleasure and *aikāne* relationships were anathema to the missionaries and the missionary-influenced Kaʻahumanu entourage of Native Hawaiians.

By the 1830s, however, Kaʻahumanu's vice grip on the kingdom had slipped substantially; the next major death among the Maui *aliʻi* was hers, in 1832. During much of that year, she had been basking in Lahaina, but she returned to Oʻahu to die at her cool country home in Mānoa Valley. Her funeral was held at the new Kawai-a-Haʻo Church. She was buried at the Royal Tomb at Pohukaina (ʻIolani Palace) and eventually transferred to Mauna ʻAla in Nuʻuanu.[105]

Upon reaching an emancipation with Kaʻahumanu's death, the king's response to the prior usurpation of his rights was to break all her introduced *kapu*. In this sense, he was a traditionalist and *pono* to the ancient ways of the *aliʻi nui*. The missionaries considered him a reactionary and attempted to encumber him with endless blame and torrents of guilt. Many of the ancient Hawaiian religious practices continued underground, however, including the veneration of various *ʻaumākua*, including the powerful *moʻo*. It is known from the missionaries that Nāhiʻenaʻena sometimes practiced the ancient religion; it is not known if Kauikeaouli did so overtly. The death of the supremely confident *kuhina nui* Kaʻahumanu empowered Kauikeaouli to take the first steps toward restoring his ancient rights. This action became known as the King's Rebellion.[106] On Oʻahu, one of his first acts after the death of Kaʻahumanu was to proclaim his *aikāne* Kaomi, a stunningly handsome half-Tahitian, joint ruler (*mōʻī kuʻi*, "engrafted king")—a move that outraged the missionaries and some of the more westernized *aliʻi nui*.

Kaomi had learned something of the art of healing from another "renegade" chief, the late Governor Boki. The catlike Kaomi, who was also expert in telling jokes and amusing the court, was at the head of a group of dandies known as the Hulumanu.[107] Initially the "engrafted king" was all-powerful. During his period of influence, a certain flavor of the ways of old returned to Oʻahu; "in Honolulu, lips smacked over the flesh of baked dog." Liquor, tobacco, and the banned hula came back. Young Kauikeaouli was winning; none of the chiefs were powerful enough to turn him away from Kaomi. Princess Nāhiʻenaʻena, who loved her brother in her own way, nearly convinced Kauikeaouli to come and live with her on Maui, but for mysterious reasons he gave her the slip on the way to the boat in Honolulu harbor at the last moment.

Rumor then reached Maui that it would now be the king's pleasure to appoint the young Liliha, Boki's beautiful widow and daughter of Hoapili, as *kuhina nui* and governor of O'ahu. Another favorite of the king, Liliha, previously dispossessed by Ka'ahumanu, was to be assisted by Chief Abner Pākī. Alarmed at the sudden élan of his charge, Hoapili rushed from Lahaina to confront Kauikeaouli on O'ahu. The king ultimately relented before his stepfather and the rebellion was over. The king's half-sister, the non-*kapu* and very piously Christian Kīna'u, would become premier. Her husband, Kekūanāo'a, a tough young chief of more humble origins, became the governor of O'ahu and commander of the military forces of the kingdom.

The king fought back, albeit passively. Kauikeaouli increasingly reacted to this loss of real political power by flaunting his traditional symbolic and social prerogatives in the spirit of the licentiousness of the Makahiki, which included cavorting with numerous female and male intimates and drinking alcoholic spirits and '*awa*.

Again with the meddling of Hoapili, the "disorder" of the king's rebellion was eventually suppressed. Liquor stills were broken up throughout the countryside. Kaomi was arrested by the king's old *kahu,* the former *kahuna* Kaikio'ewa, and was hauled before *kuhina nui* Kīna'u at the fort in Honolulu. When Kauikeaouli arrived at Kīna'u's residence, the *kahu* physically attacked him and actually wrestled the sacred king to the floor over the matter of Kaomi. Although Kaomi was subsequently released, it was the end of the career of this head bird-feather. He retreated to Kauikeaouli's palace at Kahale'uluhe in Honolulu, now thrown under a *kapu* by the king.[108] Kaomi mysteriously died a short time later.

Kauikeaouli sought solace from the Kaomi episode with his sister, who was at the time heiress apparent to the kingdom. In November 1835, Princess Nāhi'ena'ena was married off to her nephew, Leleiōhoku, son of Kamehameha I's daughter Kiliwehi and Kalanimoku at Waine'e Church in Lahaina.[109] She moved to Waikīkī on O'ahu, becoming pregnant by either Leleiōhoku or her brother the king in early 1836; it was actually a *punalua* relationship. As it became clear that Kauikeaouli was cohabiting with his beloved sister, William Richards, the enraged Christian minister and teacher of the princess, wrote from Lahaina. He went to the tomb of Keōpūolani and penned Nāhi'ena'ena a long letter, reminding her of her mother's closing days and of her hopes for her errant daughter.[110] It was superb theater: Richards, the princess's new spiritual guide, '*aumakua,* was attempting to usurp the influence of Kihawahine from the very grave of Keōpūolani.

Kamakau is discretely silent on the episode, but T. C. B. Rooke and others privy to Kauikeaouli's private life indicate that the king had formally cohabited with Nāhi'ena'ena at Pu'uloa in 'Ewa, "in a Public Manner before the chiefs at Pearl River."[111] The *pi'o* union was thus acknowledged by his supporting chiefs. Earlier, when reproached by *kuhina nui* Kīna'u over this affair with Nāhi'ena'ena,

Kauikeaouli attempted suicide. Kamakau and other missionary-influenced writers disputed the allegations that Nāhi'ena'ena's child was sired by the king. In fact, the king's relationship with his sister caused one of the biggest cover-ups in Hawaiian history. This was a traditional *pi'o* consummation that could have challenged the Christian *ali'i*'s newly discovered political powers in the kingdom.

Later in 1836, Nāhi'ena'ena was delivered of a premature, sickly child who died shortly thereafter. The princess never recovered and died near Kahale'uluhe Palace on O'ahu on 30 December 1836.

The loss of his *aikāne* Kaomi and his beloved sister Nāhi'ena'ena were not only profound shocks to Kauikeaouli personally but were affronts to the traditionally sacred status and prerogatives of a divine Hawaiian king and an insult upon his legitimate right to rule. Much as it is in the contemporary West, royal Hawaiian sexuality was an important matter to the government and the people alike. As anthropologist Marshall Sahlins has commented, the structure of the traditional Hawaiian kingdom itself existed as a "sublimated form of the forces of sexual attraction."[112] Historical events played out amidst the constant tension between primal separation of forces and their reunion. This is clearly evident in the Kumulipo legend of creation and its reenactment throughout the centuries by *ali'i*. There was nothing subliminal, however, about the drama of the royal copulation set before the assembled chiefs at Pu'uloa. To understand the mind and actions of Kauikeaouli through these suspenseful times is to begin to understand Hawaiian tradition as it existed before the historiographic editing of missionary and missionary-trained scholars.[113]

In early 1837 grief stricken Kauikeaouli prepared for his sister's funeral in Lahaina, her principal home. Portentous for the cult of the dead the king would establish around his sister, the *Sandwich Islands Gazette* reported, "Since our last the Princess has departed this life; she has not yet been entombed, as it seems to be the desire of his Majesty that she shall not be removed from his sight so long as it may be possible to prevent."[114] For the next eight years she would literally not be removed from his sight. He would take up residence at her tomb at Moku'ula.

In early 1837 a stately funeral procession wound its way through the town of Lahaina, Nāhi'ena'ena's coffin moving "down the sluice gate of Mokuhinia, and down to Halehuki, called also Halepiula."[115] This account is supported by a missionary letter: "[Nāhi'ena'ena's remains] will be deposited, together with those of her mother, Keopuolani, in the large stone building [the] property of the late Princess."[116] This is the stone tomb at Pā Halekamani. The princess would remain at the old tomb built for her mother Keōpūolani only long enough for the mausoleum at Moku'ula to be built. The first Christian tomb was emptied of its august contents (Table 1) and moved to the sacred island just as soon as Nāhi'ena'ena's stone house could be completed.

Table 1
Royal Burials at Halekamani

Individual	Rank	Relationship	Death
Keōpūolani	*ni'aupi'o* chiefess	great-granddaughter of Kekaulike wife of Kamehameha I mother of Kamehameha II, III, and Nāhi'ena'ena	1823
Kaumuali'i	king of Kaua'i	husband of Ka'ahumanu	1824
Wahine Pi'o	governor of Maui	granddaughter of Kekaulike sister of Boki and Kalanimōkū	1826
Kailikauoha	*ali'i nui*	daughter of Kahekili II wife of Hoapili mother of Liliha	1826
Kiliwehi	*ali'i nui*	daughter of Kamehameha I	late 1820s
Kaiko'olani	*ali'i nui*	son of Kamehameha I	late 1820s
Nāhi'ena'ena	*ali'i akua*	daughter of Kamehameha I	1836

A Tomb and Residence Established at Moku'ula

"Down the sluice gate of Mokuhinia, and down to Halehuki, called also Halepi-ula": these simple words describing the funeral procession of Nāhi'ena'ena are extraordinarily significant when one recalls that Kamakau also recorded that the great Maui king Pi'ilani's residence in Lahaina was Halehuki.[117] King Kamehameha III's palatial complex at Lahaina, consisting of the beachfront buildings of Hale Piula and the fishpond island of Moku'ula, is almost certainly the ancient residential site of the seventeenth-century Maui king and his family, which includes his deified daughter, Kalā'aiheana Kihawahine, and their descendants. It appears that Nāhi'ena'ena's tomb on Moku'ula was the stone house and enclosure that she had been constructing on the island sometime after the death of Governess Wahine Pi'o in 1826. The fact that Kauikeaouli did not bury her directly indicates that he may have needed time to finish or remodel the building as a tomb.

The spot selected by Kauikeaouli for his relatively permanent capital, the very grotto of Kihawahine, supplies significant evidence that the influence of the *mo'o* continued long after the destruction of more visible signs of traditional Hawaiian religious beliefs in 1819. It was not mere coincidence that a willful Nāhi'ena'ena chose to reside on the island permanently, nor was it a serendipitous place for her entombment. The king himself did not take up residence on Moku'ula solely because of the love for his departed sister.

As Kauikeaouli became more or less fixated on a single site for his royal residence, his ancestral guardian Kihawahine remained in the pond of Mokuhinia, according to traditionalists. One can hardly fail to note the resemblance between this Hawaiian "fixation" of a lizard goddess to a single locus and Apollo's impalement of the Python at Delphi, the center of that world. Valerio Valeri suggests that the close traditional association of the *mo'o* deities with foreign-introduced scrofulous diseases and fevers in the nineteenth century may account for the increasing importance of their propitiation in this troubled period.[118] *Mo'o* were often the cause, but also the cure, of many of these ailments. Disease no doubt compounded the wholesale political and cultural fragmentation of Hawaiian society in the early to mid-nineteenth century. The devastating effect of most culture contact, accompanied by introduced disease and sociopolitical and economic disruption, classically provides the foundations for revitalization movements around the world.[119] It is theorized that just that sort of phenomenon was occurring at Loko o Mokuhinia from the 1820s to the 1840s.

Kauikeaouli was at the end of a line of divine, illustrious ancestors. His home at Moku'ula served as a bridge between the dying light of Hawaiian antiquity and the challenges of a rapidly westernizing society. He and his sister, being the products of generations of *pi'o* matings, were especially concentrated "vessels" of *mana*. They would be the ultimate Hawaiian *ali'i* to attempt to replicate the system; to a large extent, the mortuary and residential complex at Moku'ula was established as a memorial to their *mana*. Now the king seemingly transformed himself in this secluded complex.

According to Kamakau, at the death of Nāhi'ena'ena the recalcitrant king disclaimed his evil ways and decided to live according to the Christian concept of righteousness. In February 1837, Kauikeaouli married Hazeleleponi Kalama Kapakuhaili, daughter of I'ahu'ula, a Hawai'i chiefess, and Nāihekukui, Kamehameha I's ship captain. Kalama was additionally the *hānai* daughter of Miriam Kekāuluohi and Charles Kana'ina.[120] The abolition of the *kapu* system did not anticipate abolition of class distinction, however. The king's marriage to Kalama, a chiefess of decidedly lesser rank and considered a *kaukau ali'i* by many, was a resounding slap in the face of the Christian powers—including the Christian *ali'i nui* who could not tolerate his traditional duty and right to have a *pi'o* child with his sister. If he could not have the highest traditionally ranked female, he would choose according to love regardless of social standing. One could imagine that Kauikeaouli's act was almost a rite of reversal, but for the fact that Kalama was hardly a commoner.

Although Kamakau portrays Kauikeaouli as living quietly and righteously with Kalama in the calm of Mokuhinia, firsthand accounts portray a rather unrecalcitrant king. The eagle eye of stepfather Hoapili (Figure 12) was a stone's throw away, on the eastern shore of Mokuhinia at Kuloloia. The nearby bells of Waineʻe Church pealed in vain upon Kauikeaouli's resolve. The king was able at last to lead a traditional, albeit somewhat penurious, life as a Hawaiian *mōʻī* on Mokuʻula. In fact, some of his Hulumanu from the wild days in Oʻahu accompanied him. The residences of many of the courtiers in Lahaina, Hulumanu and otherwise, were close at hand, just to the north of Mokuʻula at the enclosure of Pākalā within Kaluaʻehu. Here were Abner Pākī, of the rebellious Liliha/Boki *mā,* and the homes of his closest childhood friends: Fanny Young and husband George Naʻea, Joshua Kaʻeo and wife Gini Lahilahi Young, *aikāne* Keoni Ana (John Young II), and the king's secretary and *aikāne,* Timothy Haʻalilio (Figure 13). The children of Kamehameha I's English military advisor, John Young, were *hapa* (half) Hawaiian and blood cousins of Kauikeaouli. Haʻalilio was half-brother of Levi Haʻalelea, Kekauʻōnohi's husband and heir. Haʻalilio's uncle was Native Hawaiian historian David Malo.[121]

The king needed a refuge from internal conflict. Despite the fact that Hoapili, Kīnaʻu, and other Native Hawaiian *aliʻi* supporters of the Christian mission were often more in control of the reigns of the kingdom and subscribed to a Calvinist

Figure 12. Ulumaheiheihoapili in 1837. Born of royal Maui heritage, he was Kamehameha I's closest friend and hereditary guardian and high priest of the *moʻo* Kihawahine. He became a Christian and later the husband of Keōpūolani and governor of Maui. Bishop Museum CP 76807.

Figure 13. Timothy Haʻalilio, ca. 1830s. He was Kamehameha III's personal secretary and advisor. Bishop Museum CP 117,133.

Christian culture, these individuals also constituted Kauikeaouli's family. Out of the respect and love he must have felt for many members of his extended royal family, he seems to have often mounted only passive resistance, especially after the losses of Kaomi and Nāhiʻenaʻena. The private world of Mokuʻula represented a resistance through retreat.

One of the most vivid descriptions of the tomb and residence at Mokuʻula soon after its establishment is that of Andelusia Lee Conde, a missionary who wrote of Kauikeaouli's personal cult of the royal dead in 1837:[122]

> Went with my husband today to call upon the king. He occupies a large stone building rather splendid in its appearance. We were met at the door by His Majesty and very politely invited to walk in. A large armed chair was ordered for me and Mr. C. was seated upon a sofa by his Majesty's side. He was very sociable and kind and appeared quite interesting. We were also escorted by himself alone to the chamber where were deposited the remains of his deceased mother and sister the young princess and his sister's child. The room was a large chamber elegantly furnished with chairs, tables with large mirrors set under them, beautiful china matting and a small organ upon which he played for our entertainment. Nearly in the centre of the room was placed a bedstead nearly the magnitude of 3 common bedsteads. Upon which was a bed neatly spread, and upon this were placed the three coffins, side by side, mostly splendidly ornamented. Each of these corpses were enclosed in 3 coffins—the first zinc— the second lead and the third or outside one, of wood. These were covered with scarlet silk velvet, put on with a multitude of brass nails— gilded plates, with their names & c. upon them, and various gilded ornaments, that gave us almost any impression but that of a tomb. These coffins are covered first by a black figured gauze having spread sufficiently large, to cover the bed and nearly to the floor. This was covered by another of the same kind, of a delicate peach blow color, both also surrounded by a deep blue mosquito net of Chinese manufacture. Without this, around the bed were stationed several kahilis like so many tall sentinels to keep unceasing vigils over the dead. Some of these were not more than 4 feet long, and no longer than common fly brushes, others extended to the floor above, and were as large around as a mans boddy; and very curiously made, the feathers being wound upon the staff. Some of these were red, some green, some yellow, and others black, some were veragated. In a small cupboard with glass doors were deposited articles of very rich and splendid dress formerly worn by the Princess. These consisted of black lace embroidered with silk of various colors—silk velvets ornamented with tinsel cord and gold lace, a beautiful white satin cape

very richly ornamented, and some other things. This splendid room opened into a piazza that commanded a fine view of the harbour.

Despite being awed by the splendor of the tomb and the exquisite taste of her erstwhile host, Conde, remembering her Calvinist training, did not overlook Kauikeaouli's fondness for spirit and the flesh: "The king was gentlemanly in his manners and his house rather splendid, but alas! for the mind degenerated, ruined by intemperance and vice!"

A while later, Mary Ives recorded a similar spectacle:[123]

> A few days since Mr. I. and myself called on the king and requested to see the tomb of the princess Harrietta [Nāhiʻenaʻena]. He showed us into a chamber elegantly furnished in which was a bedstead twice as long as common ones, covered with a rich bedspread—large and elegant kahilies, ten or twelve feet high stood around the bed. The king drew off the spread and there stood three coffins, covered on the outside with scarlet silk velvet and ornamented with brasses and brass nails. It was indeed a splendid sight. I could not realize I was in a sepulchre altho they were shaped like coffins. I could not feel that such splendor covered the deformities of the dead. The coffin in the centre contained the remains of the princess; that on the right hand her mother and the one on the left her child. The kahilies were formed like a trooper's feather; were made of small feathers of different colors and were as large around as my body. Near the bed stood a glass cupboard containing some articles of dress belonging to the princess among which were several pairs of satin shoes of various colors, a large black lace veil embroidered with pink roses with green leaves, some other things embossed with gold and silver tinsel. They are now preparing to celebrate the anniversary of her death & have sent a vessel to another Island to obtain hogs & other things.

And, in the style of a good missionary housewife, Ives added: "Yesterday I had the honor of directing the king's men and women in making the cake."

The closing years of the 1830s saw the death of Kauikeaouli's stepsister Liliha, a granddaughter of Kahekili who had been humiliated by Kaʻahumanu and Kīnaʻu, banished from the court, and disenfranchised—thus a perfect soul mate to the king and beloved by the *makaʻāinana*. Kamakau claims that bold chief Boki's widow, dying at the age of 37, had been poisoned. "[Liliha's] body was sent back to Mokuʻula at Lahaina on Maui and placed with that of the princess Harriet Nahiʻenaʻena, and chiefs and commoners bewailed her life with a sorrow that abides in the hearts of many."[124]

The 1830s were described by Kamakau and many Western writers as a period of disorder. It is clear, however, that it was a time for Native Hawaiians to attempt to revive their fractured culture. Kauikeaouli's actions in attempting to depose the power of the female *kuhina nui,* his support of Liliha, his union with his sister Nāhiʻenaʻena, his marriage with the "mere" kaukau *aliʻi* Kalama, his general revelry, his *aikāne,* his move to Mokuʻula and the establishment of the tomb there—all are indicative of a king trying to reclaim traditional rights and prerogatives of an indigenous ruler. It was a message not lost upon his people—the 1830s was a time of attempted revitalization.

Richards and other missionaries in Hawaiʻi were well aware of this situation, and a general letter was published in the *Missionary Herald* in Boston:[125] "Circumstances of a local nature are such as the turning of some of the people to their ancient customs at Honolulu, the defection of a part of the church at Kailua, and the turning of a party to idolatry at Hilo." It was added that the Hawaiians were backsliding into sin as a "dog returneth to his vomit." W. D. Alexander commented that "the ancient idolatry was still cherished by many in secret, and their hereditary superstitions, hydra-headed in their variety and tenacity of life, were destined to survive for generations to come, and necessarily blended with and colored their conceptions of Christianity."[126]

The traditional religious revival is linked to Kauikeaouli's rebellion of the 1830s. It was described by Sahlins as the "first of a series of social movements by which the people-in-general demonstrated their disenchantment with the powers-that-be."[127] Mokuʻula became a symbol of the traditional source of ascendancy, Waineʻe Church the usurper. Cycles of traditional and Christian *mana* alternated rapidly during these years. Certain aspects of the ancient religion, especially sorcery (and Kihawahine was a major sorcery deity) were returning.[128]

Within this context of vibrant revitalization and the agonies of the formerly divine king, it is not surprising that the *moʻo* Mokuhinia (Kihawahine) was sighted at Loko o Mokuhinia and at other locations throughout this time. The most famous spectacle was in 1838, when Auhea Miriam Kekāuluohi, soon to be appointed *kuhina nui* at the death of Kīnaʻu, was nearly tossed into the black waters of Mokuhinia by the giant lizard. The chiefess had been canoeing across the waters on her way to church at Waineʻe.[129]

The revival of certain traditional Native Hawaiian religious practices was met with Christian fanaticism, too. The supernatural appearance of Kihawahine can be viewed as an aspect of the Christian revivalistic social movement known as the "Great Awakening," which had recently spread to Maui from its origin on Oʻahu.[130] The populist movement revolved around the theme of personal Christian salvation and was accompanied with wailings, faintings, visions, and general hysteria. It followed a few years after the king's failed rebellion against the new Christian powers. The miraculous appearance of the goddess Kihawahine Mokuhinia and her aggression toward a devout Christian chiefess symbolized to the participants the last gasp of power of the old religion and the traditional legitimacy of its divine king living at Kalua o Kiha.

Kekāuluohi, the "Big-Mouth Queen"

Perhaps the rising star of Auhea Miriam Kekāuluohi (Figure 14) had a particular importance to the happenings at Loko o Mokuhinia, beyond being nearly dunked into its waters. By many accounts, Kekāuluohi, daughter of Hoapili's wife Kahei-heimālia, was an impressive figure. She was intimately involved with popularizing the Christian church and eventually wrenching control over Kalua o Kiha from her own stepfather Hoapili. Like many of the *ali'i nui wahine,* this niece of the imperious Ka'ahumanu had an outstanding physical presence:

> This lady is upwards of six feet in height; her frame is exceedingly large and well covered with fat. She was dressed in yellow silk, with enormously large gigot sleeves, and wore on her head a tiara of beautiful yellow feathers interspersed with a few of a scarlet colour. Above the feathers appeared a large tortoise-shell comb, that confined her straight black hair. Her shoulders were covered with a richly embroidered shawl of scarlet crape. She sat in a large arm-chair, over which was thrown a robe made of the same kind of yellow feathers as decked her tiara. Her feet were encased in white cotton stockings and men's shoes. She was altogether one of the most remarkable looking personages I have ever seen.[131]

At the time of her near-capsizing, the missionaries' sweetheart Kekāuluohi was in charge of the lands of Mokuhinia, the *'āina* under the traditional guardianship of the *mo'o* Kihawahine. One can speculate why Kekāuluohi was the major

Figure 14. Auhea Miriam Kekāuluohi. Engraving by Welsh and Walter after A. T. Agate, 1845. Bishop Museum CP 104,180.

object of *mo'o* wrath during this time of mass hysteria. First, Kekāuluohi, along with her mother Kaheiheimālia, Keōpūolani, and Ka'ahumanu, was instrumental in overthrowing the *'aikapu,* the prohibition against women eating with men. She was said to be the first *ali'i* woman to eat consecrated pork from the *heiau,* the first to commit the sacrilege. The high drama of Ka'ahumanu and Keōpūolani convincing Liholiho to eat with them followed shortly thereafter. Second, Kekāuluohi, who came to be known as the "Big-Mouth Queen," had been the first to accept the Protestant faith of the missionaries. Kekāuluohi was among the most active in the support of the mission and Waine'e Church specifically, together with her mother and stepfather. Third, Kekāuluohi, as heiress to her half-sister Kīna'u in land and position, represented the succession of the powerful *wahine* lineage of *kūhina nui* established by Ka'ahumanu. When Ka'ahumanu could not provide offspring to Kamehameha I from her royal Maui lineage, her sister Kaheiheimālia did so through their daughter Kahō'anokū Kīna'u. Another daughter of Kaheiheimālia, Kekāuluohi, was provided by Kamehameha's half-brother Kalaimamahū.[132]

Kekāuluohi was an agent of the new Christian missionaries, who had supported the continuation of the *kuhina nui* co-rulership. Sometimes referred to as Ka'ahumanu III, she was a true sister of her predecessor Kīna'u, who was likewise attentive to the domestic missives of the beaming missionary wives: "I should like to take my friends to the dwelling-house of our premier, Kinau, that they might see how well she arranges her domestic affairs. I have had one of her attendants in training several months. She has learned to make bread, cake, custards, and puddings."[133]

A fourth possible motivation for traditionalist criticism in the form of a *mo'o* sighting stems from Kekāuluohi's position as principal *konohiki* for many of the lands of *ali'i nui* who had died and left their lands to the children of her sister Kīna'u. This probably included Waine'e *ahupua'a,* which contained Loko o Mokuhinia and Moku'ula. Kīna'u died in 1839, followed by Hoapili, Liliha, and several other *ali'i nui.* The death of so many chiefs had the effect of ending the Great Awakening of Christian revival, but not the grasping for land and power by Kekāuluohi and other survivors.

The Royal Court of Lahaina in the Early 1840s

The inner court of King Kamehameha III at Moku'ula became a tight, defensive group against the admonitions of the missionaries and their new Christian converts, who were now becoming a sizable part of the population. The Great Christian Awakening of the late 1830s could have pushed nominally Christian Kauikeaouli and his immediate court further into seclusion on his little island. Although we cannot be sure of the king's defensive attitude toward the outside, we are reasonably sure that internal life on Moku'ula was relatively more free-spirited than that found in zealous Christian circles.

After the death of Hoapili and other *ali'i nui* in 1840 and the end of the Christian revival, there was a general relaxation of Christian prohibitions (the blue laws) first established by Ka'ahumanu. This was accompanied by a rise in *noa* (free) living that no doubt Kauikeaouli relished. His court in the early 1840s was beginning to burst with activity that would likely embarrass the more prudential missionaries.

The early 1840s was also a good time for the transition of the government from an absolute monarchy (actually a dyarchy with the *kuhina nui*) to a constitutional form. The missionary William Richards developed a bill of rights in 1839, and in 1840 his constitution was promulgated in Lahaina. It called for an executive consisting of the king and *kuhina nui,* a two-house legislature of an *ali'i* assembly and one popularly elected, and a judiciary.[134] The *kuhina nui* maintained her establishment on Honolulu, but the rest of the government was centered at the royal complex of Moku'ula and Hale Piula.

Despite the carefree style, domestic life at Moku'ula was not without fretful moments of jealousy. Just after the birth of the king's son Keaweawe'ulaokalani I by Queen Kalama, cousin Keoni Ana was caught in Kalama's bedroom by the king. Enraged, the king ordered a black flag of death to be raised above Lahaina. Kamehameha III went into retreat. Kalama and Keoni Ana's wife Julia Alapa'i Kauwā lived anxious hours "day and night outside the enclosure of Moku'ula," while the chiefs gathered at adjacent Hale Piula to debate the king's death sentence. Kaheiheimālia Hoapiliwahine was brought in to convince the king to spare Keoni Ana's life. The king relented.[135]

Rumor correctly predicted that Keoni Ana would become the king's favorite. He relented indeed. A few months later, after the death of Hoapili in 1840, he succeeded in appointing his new *aikāne,* Keoni Ana, governor of Maui; he also succeeded in sharing Keoni Ana's wife Julia Alapa'i and taking Keoni Ana's sister Gini Lahilahi Young as mistress.[136]

Kauikeaouli had twin boys with Gini Lahilahi: Kīwala'ō, who died at birth, and Albert Kūnuiākea Kūkā'ilimoku, who would live to 1903. Although a *hānai* son to Queen Kalama, Albert would suffer the indignity of an illegitimate birth in a Calvinist Christian Hawai'i. This son, most likely the last grandson of Kamehameha I, the ultimate of his line, served his kingdom as House representative in 1880.[137]

Kauikeaouli's two infant sons by Kalama also died in infancy, sometime between 1839 and 1842. The second child was given in *hānai* to Kaheiheimālia but soon developed a fever and died, at the age of only 31 days. Dr. Baldwin of Lahaina was convinced that the child was killed by traditional medicinal treatment.[138] Keaweaweʻulaokalani I and II were among the last immediate family members of Kamehameha III to be interred at Mokuʻula. According to one source, Hoapili and Kaheiheimālia, who also died during this period, were buried at Mokuʻula as well.[139]

The type of relationship shared by Kauikeaouli, Alapaʻi, Keoni Ana, and Kalama was the traditional *punalua,* "two springs," practiced by chiefs of old. The *aikāne* affiliation of Kauikeaouli with Kaomi, Keoni Ana, and others had been practiced by Kalaniʻōpuʻu, Kamehameha, Kahekili, and other great *mōʻī* as yet another mark of their exalted *aliʻi* status. Thus a major component of the lifestyle of the royal household at Mokuʻula was traditional. The conventional royal marriage practices of *punalua, piʻo,* and *aikāne* would pass into history with Kamehameha III's death.

Kamehameha III and Kalama settled into a comfortable domestic life within the *kapu* enclosure of Mokuʻula, most likely in *hale pili* next to the large, two-story stone tomb of his sister and mother. Keoni Ana and Julia Alapaʻi had become their closest intimates. Charles Wilkes visited Lahaina in the early 1840s, during the time the Western-style "palace" at Hale Piula was being built, and provided not only a general account of the town of Lahaina but perhaps the most detailed account of life at Mokuʻula.[140] This account is quite illustrative of the changing economy of the Hawaiian Islands:

> The king's palace [Hale Piula] is built of coral rock, and is only half-finished: it already seems to be in a somewhat dilapidated state, and exhibits poverty rather than regal magnificence. His present residence is neither calculated to maintain the respect of his subjects, nor to enhance his importance in the eyes of foreigners. The town of Lahaina is built along the beach for a distance of three-quarters of a mile: it is principally composed of grass houses, situated as near the beach as possible: it has one principal street with a few others running at right angles. After the king's palace, the fort is the most conspicuous object: its form is quadrangular. The longest side, facing the sea: it is of little account, however, as a defense, serving chiefly to confine unruly subjects and sailors in. The area within is about one acre, and the wall are twenty feet high.... There are store houses, which are used for the reception of the king's revenue that consists of large heaps of tapas. Instead of being received in the dilapidated and half-finished palace, I was ushered over a small causeway to a short distance behind it into his private apartments, and introduced to his wife, who had been quite unwell. She is not acknowledged as queen. She is the daughter of an inferior chief on the island of Hawaii, and the prettiest woman on the island. The king, it is believed, married her from affection, and against the wishes of his chiefs, after they had prohibited

his marriage with his sister Nahienaena. After crossing the causeway we reached a small island: on this was a grass-house of moderate dimensions, surrounded by hibiscus trees, which grow quite low, and made a bower almost impervious to the sun's rays. At the entrance to the house I was met by his Majesty, dressed in a round about of blue cloth, and white pantaloons. He led the way into the bower, in the center of which his wife was lying in a clean white hammock, suspended between the trees. Everything about her was pleasant looking, betakening care and attention to her comfort, and a degree of refinement I little expected to see. Although unwell, she showed many marks of beauty and I was much struck with her appearance. The king told me these were his private apartments where they could remain undisturbed and free from intrusion. They passed most of their time there together, and he pointed out a small hut of tea [ti] leaves that he had constructed for her, in which she had been lying on new-mown grass. The king pointed out the improvements he had in contemplation but complained that he had not money to carry them on. Although his income is very considerable, in tapas and native produce, & would have constituted great wealth in former times, yet, from the depreciation in the value of the articles, it is now of little value. He has so many hangers-on that it takes a large amount to supply, maintain, and clothe them. These circumstances leave the king quite as poor as any of his subjects.

That Kauikeaouli had suffered a notorious reputation, in the world of the missionaries and their zealous converts in the powerful Ka'ahumanu and Kīna'u *mā*, is seen in the surprise of Wilkes:

> The little domestic scene I had witnessed gave me a great pleasure, the more from being quite unexpected, and I found afterwards that very few are ever admitted to this sanctum sanctorum. I take pleasure in mentioning it, as I had not before given his Majesty credit for the domestic virtues, which I am now satisfied he possesses to a great degree, both from the tenor of his conversation and the pleasing picture he exhibited in the last interview I had with him.

Wilkes continued to be impressed with the attractiveness of Queen Kalama, who had been shunned by many in court: "His wife is much fairer than the natives usually and she had not so coarse and disproportionate a figure as seems characteristic of the females of distinction in these islands. Her features, however, were decidedly of the Native character. The tone of the voice was pleasing and lady-like."

Other writers were not so kind with the "sprightly" Queen Kalama. Along with her husband, she liked to drink. "The Queen had been tried by the church for *'awa* drinking"[141]—a statement demonstrative of the extent of abuse the foreign missionaries were inflicting upon the Hawaiian people. The "naughty" wife of Kamehameha III, who was anything but colorless, had her small moments of revenge: "Queen Kalama attended a 'teetotal' party at the Judd's in 1846 and in a 'superb gesture of disdain spat out a mouthful of tea onto the hall floor with an explosion as were it the spouting of a large fish.'"[142]

Despite Queen Kalama's eagerness to fit into the missionary ideal, she was still snubbed by many of the *ali'i nui*. Laura Fish Judd wrote on the friction in the royal household between *hānai* mother and daughter:

> The old premier [Kekāuluohi] was a little jealous of the queen, being her superior by birth, and when I made purchases for them, I was always obliged to allow the old lady the first choice. She always wanted her sash a little longer and her bows a little larger than the queen's. And because the latter was young and had pretty hair, which she wore in ringlets, why, the dear old premier must have hers curled too, which made her a little ridiculous, yet she was really good and tried to be an exemplary Christian.[143]

The American merchant Gorham Gilman, long-time resident of Lahaina, recorded his impressions of a comfortable Moku'ula in the early 1840s:

> Again passing across the street we come to a narrow causeway across which a little gate is constructed, so that passing is prevented unless by permission of the sentry of the king who has charge of the royal premises. The buildings occupied by the king are in keeping with most of the other large, fine thatched houses with modern conveniences for comfort and with a certain lanai or kind of canopy made of cocoanut leaves and natural vines.[144]

George Simpson visited Moku'ula in 1841–42, calling upon Kauikeaouli and two of his Hulumanu, Timothy Ha'alilio, his private secretary and treasurer, and Keoni Ana, his chamberlain and governor of Maui:[145]

> From the chapel we went to the palace [either Moku'ula or Hale Piula], which, like some other residence of royalty, is badly situated, occupying a low spot around stagnant patches of kalo. The sentries on duty, who were neatly dressed in white uniforms, saluted us as we passed. In point of stature and carriage, they would have bourne a comparison ... with our finest grenadiers. At the entrance we were met by the king, accompanied by Haalilio, his secretary, and Keoni Ana, chamberlain of the establishment, and governor of the island, all three wearing the Windsor uniform and appearing to be much about the same age, probably under thirty. Kauikeaouli is very dark; he is, however, good-humored and well

formed, and speaks very tolerable English. Haalilio … had a countenance of considerable intelligence and to my personal knowledge, did not belie his looks in that respect.

Not missing an opportunity to point out the presumed superiority of his own Western civilization, Simpson continued his Victorian circumlocutions:

> Keoni Ana, according to the principles of enunciation as developed under a former head, is the Hawaiian disguise for John Young, the present bearer of the appellation being son and namesake of the common sailor … whom Kamehameha elevated, as a monument of the immeasurable superiority of the rudest civilization over every form of savage life, to be governor of his native island, and vice roy of all chiefs. If inferior to his father in mental qualities, Keoni Ana possesses a good face and handsome figure. And the three companions welcomed us with a cordial shake of hand and expressed their gratification at seeing us, they were fluent in their elocution, and easy & graceful in their manners.

Simpson was then led over to the tomb at Mokuʻula:

> His Majesty offered us everything which he deemed conducive to our comfort, houses, servants, boats, & c.; and, after joining us in a glass of wine, we were conducted by him to visit a kind of revival of the grand mausoleum in Honolulu, the tomb of his mother, who was one of the very earliest converts to Christianity, his first wife, who was also his sister, and his three children, all deposited in handsomely mounted coffins of native manufacture. The conversation turned on fifty different topics, in which the king was likely to take an interest, such as railroads, swimming, dancings, riding, & c.; and the whole of us speedily became excellent friends. At parting, his Majesty engaged to bring his two comrades and other principal authorities to dine on Tuesday on board of the Cowlitz.

It is interesting to note that the coffins of Liliha and the "other chiefs" were apparently not noticed by Simpson or other visitors. Perhaps they were not in the same place of honor accorded the king's immediate family—the tomb/house, by all accounts, was very large. One wonders if the glassware, liquor, and conversations about railroads were proof of the king's westernization or merely a sign of *aloha* and hospitality given to his foreign visitors. The missionary teachers, hoping to turn "savage" Hawaiians into civilized Christians, had been eagerly anticipating the former transformation.

Gilman, who had arrived in Lahaina in the early 1840s, recalls a different version of the king's life at Mokuʻula:

One day I heard some people singing coming up the road, and stepping to the veranda I saw a small company parading the streets in a shower of rain. It was the king, and his wife, the queen, his trusty friend and official, John Young [Keoni Ana], and wife [Alapaʻi], and several others in the party. They were without shoes and stockings and hats and with a large wreath of maile and no more clothes than necessary. They were as happy as any children playing in summer showers. The company had just come from performing one of those ancient acts of community interest, teaching the people the dignity of labor. The king and his friends had a kalo patch.[146]

One could not envision a gamboling, barefooted Victoria and Albert parading around Pall Mall, nor singing Habsburgs playing leapfrog on Kardnerstrauß in Vienna. The court was enjoying their life among their people, in a manner similar to Kamehameha I.

The idea that the display of certain foreign affectations by the royal court of King Kamehameha III was designed primarily to please Westerners is further substantiated by the lack of urgency felt in the construction of the palace at Hale Piula. By 1841 the coral block mansion was still not completed, and Kauikeaouli and Kalama continued to reside in traditional accommodation at Mokuʻula. An agreement between the king and the contractor indicates that the residences on Mokuʻula, however, were slated to be upgraded: "Halstead agrees to build the stone house of the King now in course of preparation, and to complete the same and also a wooden house (mauka) above the other, such work as properly belongs to a carpenter. At the completion of the said buildings Halstead shall continue to remain in the employment of the King, six months out of each year for a term of ten years when this agreement shall terminate."[147] With an acute shortage of cash funds, these matters were clearly not priorities to the king.

Kaluaʻehu and the Great Mahele

Ironically, the first known painting of Mokuʻula, by James Sawkins in 1851 (Figure 15), and the first known maps of the palace complex at Kalua o Kiha were created several years after Kauikeaouli's court had left for Honolulu.[148] It is somewhat unusual to have early survey plans of Mokuʻula and Loko o Mokuhinia at all. Crown Lands did not have to be surveyed for they were, of course, not liable for commutation to the government or for taxation. It is fortunate that two of the most distinguished surveyors of the kingdom provided early surveys of the site.

An undated Monsarrat plan (Figure 16) and survey report that conform to the drafting style and calligraphy of Monsarrat's Great Mahele work of the late 1840s or early 1850s indicate a stone wall at the southwestern corner of the site

Figure 15. The Presbyterian Church, Lahaina. 1851. Watercolor by James Gay Sawkins. This is the only known image of the sacred island of Moku'ula (left) from the times of King Kamehameha III. Rex Nan Kivell Collection, NK6298/68, National Library of Australia.

that extends *mauka* to Front Street. Then the property line traces a causeway that became Shaw Street. The boundary follows the Waine'e Church lot to "a small pond" that is probably a *lo'i* of Ualo. Subsequently, the line turns to the west to a stone wall along Front Street. After following the road to the south, the boundary turns west to the starting point on the beach.

The beachfront of Loko o Mokuhinia is noted as "Hale Piula" on the Monsarrat map, but the structure shown is most likely not the large palace but rather the house of Napaepae that is noted in subsequent documents. Three small fishponds extend along Front Street in this parcel, including part of the fishpond sometimes referred to as Loko o Nalehu, which contains the sluice gate of Loko o Mokuhinia, and two smaller fishponds that appear to be lobes of Loko o Mokuhinia, separated only by Front Street. The aquatic connection between Loko o Mokuhinia and the sea is bridged by a small span on Front Street, just south of a short causeway that leads from Hale Piula to Moku'ula. This bridge can be seen in Sawkins's watercolor.

The tomb of the *ali'i* was on the northern part of Moku'ula. Adjacent to this structure to the west and southward along the island were originally two holding ponds within the large fishpond of Mokuhinia. Documents suggest that this was the site of the freshwater springs *(punawai)* that were the main source of water to Loko o Mokuhinia.[149] It is probable that these holding ponds were used for the collection of drinking water, for royal bathing, or for keeping choice, fresh fish for

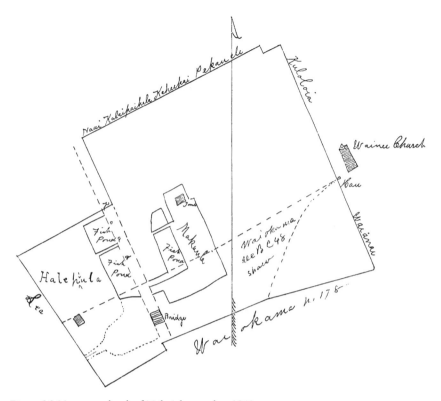

Figure 16. Monsarrat sketch of Moku'ula area, late 1840s.

the royal table. The southeast corner of the surveyed parcel was bisected by the shoreline of Mokuhinia.

The original causeway connecting Moku'ula with Front Street was about 3.4 meters wide, sufficiently broad to drive a carriage across. The island was set back far enough (14.9 meters) to have prevented people from jumping across the moat. A gate extending across the causeway was set back about 3 meters from the street, according to the Alexander survey of 1855.

The Crown parcel containing Mokuhinia, Hale Piula, and Loko o Mokuhinia extended south to what became Shaw Street according to Monsarrat's survey. An etching based on Jay Antrim's daguerreotype of 1856 is perhaps a view of the Shaw causeway to the west, with the island of Lāna'i in the background (Figure 17). Text accompanying this newspaper illustration indicates that the scene is near "one of the government palaces," perhaps Hale Piula. This southern section of Mokuhinia was later disputed by the Shaw family, owners of Waiokama *ahupua'a* (see p. 88).

Another survey of Moku'ula was completed in 1855 by W. P. Alexander after the court had left and Kamehameha III had died. Some of the island's dimensions and features had changed in the intervening years since the Monsarrat survey. In the Alexander survey, the rectilinear island appears to have been extended slightly to the north beyond the tomb. The northernmost holding tank is gone. The placement and shape of Moku'ula within Loko o Mokuhinia conform closely to a subsequent S. E. Bishop survey of 1884 (Figure 18). It is possible that data from the 1855 survey were used for the 1884 map.

Radiating outward from the center of courtly life at Moku'ula and Kalua o Kiha was the protective fishpond of Loko o Mokuhinia. Along its shoreline in the 1840s were the residences of the king's extended family, chiefs, ministers, friends, and other close associates. This region of Lahaina is generally known as Kalua'ehu. The richest source of detail concerning settlement patterns and land tenure in the Kalua'ehu is provided in the books, surveys, and testimonies gathered during the land distribution of 1848–53.[150] At the Great Mahele, Kauikeaouli first recalled all the 'āina in his own name, then redistributed it for himself and his chiefs. This act of redistribution and privatization of lands in the kingdom was based both in tradition and on the novel experience of economic monetization. It was a traditional act (kālai'āina, the returning of the land to the king), usually done on the ascension of a new king, rights denied Kauikeaouli during the rule of the female kuhina nui. It was novel in the sense that, with the Kuleana Act of 1850, commoners could manage their lands without the tenant obligations characteristic of the traditional

Figure 17. Possible view of Shaw Street looking makai toward the island of Lāna'i. From The West Side, 1856. Bishop Museum CP 96333.

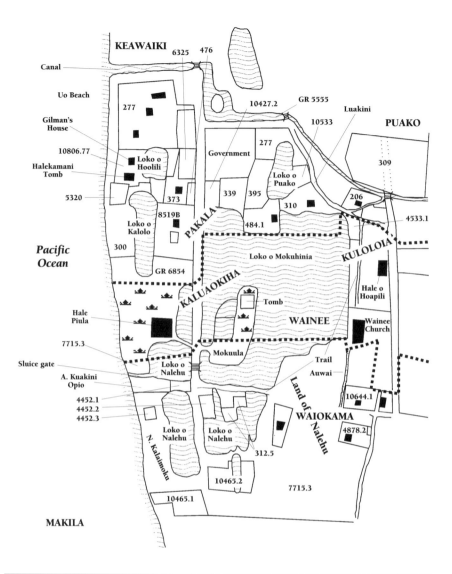

KEAWAIKI

Canal

Uo Beach

Gilman's House

10806.77

Halekamani Tomb

5320

Pacific Ocean

Hale Piula

7715.3

Sluice gate

A. Kuakini Opio

4452.1
4452.2
4452.3

MAKILA

6325   476

277

Loko o Hoolili

373   8519B

Loko o Kalolo

300

GR 6854

277

Loko o Nalehu

N. Kalaimoku

Loko o Nalehu

10465.2

10465.1

10427.2

Government

339   395

484.1

KALUAOKIHA

Mokuula

Loko o Nalehu

312.5

7715.3

GR 5555

10533

PAKALA

Loko o Puako

310

Loko o Mokuhinia

Tomb

WAINEE

Trail

Auwai

Land of Nalehu

WAIOKAMA

Luakini

PUAKO

309

206

4533.1

KULOLOIA

Hale o Hoapili

Wainee Church

10644.1

4878.2

Land Commission Awards

206	Catalina		484.1	Kaihe'ekai		8519B	Fanny Young
277	W. C. Lunalilo		4452.1	Kalama		10465.1	Nalehu
300	A. Paki		4452.2	Kalama		10465.2	Nalehu
309	D. Malo		4452.3	Kalama		10427.2	Na'ea
310	Pikanele		4533.1	Ualo		10533	Lazaro
312.5	Keaweiwi		4878.2	Upai		10644.1	Pi'iko
339	Kalapaihala		5320	A. Ka'eo		10806.77	Kamehameha III
373	La'ahili		6325	Ha'alelea		GR 5555	C. Lindsay
395	Kahikona		7715.3	Lota Kamehameha		GR 6854	V. Kamamalu
476	Pikao			to L&P Shaw in 1879			

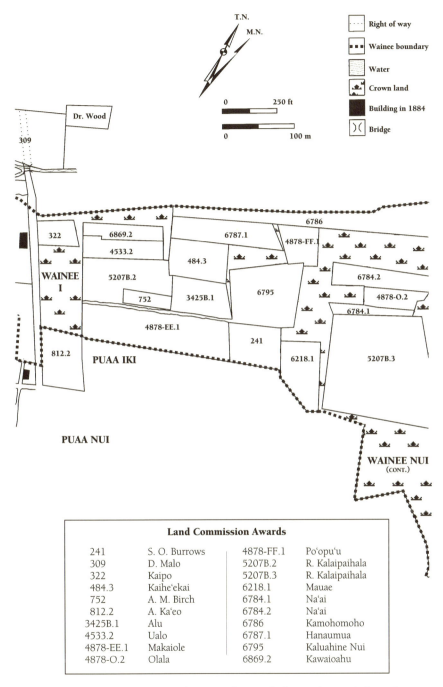

Land Commission Awards

241	S. O. Burrows	4878-FF.1	Po'opu'u
309	D. Malo	5207B.2	R. Kalaipaihala
322	Kaipo	5207B.3	R. Kalaipaihala
484.3	Kaihe'ekai	6218.1	Mauae
752	A. M. Birch	6784.1	Na'ai
812.2	A. Ka'eo	6784.2	Na'ai
3425B.1	Alu	6786	Kamohomoho
4533.2	Ualo	6787.1	Hanaumua
4878-EE.1	Makaiole	6795	Kaluahine Nui
4878-O.2	Olala	6869.2	Kawaioahu

Figure 18. Lower Waine'e *ahupua'a* in the 1840s, showing the large Loko o Mokuhinia. Reconstructed from documents of the Great Mahele of 1848–53 and S. E. Bishop survey of 1884.

konohiki system. With a subsequent Royal Patent, commoners could secure their lands in fee simple. Furthermore, it became possible for foreigners to own land.

More than any other act, however, the Mahele destroyed the traditional sociopolitical bonds linking the commoners, chiefs, and king. With the land alienated from the societal collective, the people and the chiefs were no longer bound by the socially embedded rules of mutual obligation. In a very real sense, then, Kauikeaouli was the last traditional, divine ruler of the Hawaiian Islands. An examination of the Mahele records provides a detailed survey of the traditional system of land tenure and social relationships between the chiefly households and those of the *maka'āinana* at Kalua'ehu the instant before they disappeared.

Beachfront acreage of Pākalā was a choice neighborhood inhabited by the royal court and *kaukau ali'i* (lesser chiefs) in the early days of the nineteenth century. This was anything but a typical *maka'āinana* neighborhood in 1848. The core of the *ali'i* settlement was near the beach of Pākalā, a favorite ancient surfing area known as 'Uo. Here were the houselots of the *kapu* women and powerful chiefs of the Maui and Hawai'i dynasties, once again united and amplified through the marriage of Keōpūolani and Kamehameha. Here were the homes of the influential *hapa haole* (half Caucasian) Young family.

The nucleus of this neighborhood in Kalua'ehu was part of Kamehameha I's encampment of *ali'i* of 1802. That gathering may have extended from the "Brick Palace" (near the present library) and Keaweaiki southward to Moku'ula, the Kalua o Kiha. Prior to the Mahele, O'ahu governor Kekūanāo'a was in charge of Pākalā, a duty he relinquished just prior to the Mahele in 1848 (*Mahele Book* 29).

A large section of this beach frontage was occupied by Abner Pākī, father of Princess Bernice Pauahi Bishop (LCA 300, 10:585). Occupying about half of Pākī's parcel was a large section of Loko o Ka'alolo (probably from Ka'aimalolo; also called Loko o Kekūanāo'a). The *loko* was most likely a sand-banked pond *(loko pu'uone)* characteristic of Mokuhinia and surrounding ponds. A small lot for Asa Ka'eo, brother/cousin to Pākī through Ka'eo's mother Ka'aimalolo, was just to the north along the beach (LCA 5320). Asa was a *kahili* bearer for Kauikeaouli.[151] North of Gilman's "Seaside Cottage," as he named Nāhi'ena'ena's *hale pili* Halekamani, were lands extending to Canal Street—another parcel of the original royal compound. Here was the house of Charles Kana'ina and *kuhina nui* Auhea Miriam Kekāuluohi, parents of future King William Charles Lunalilo: "Among the most pretentious [of chiefly houses at this location] was that of the ex-queen of Kamehameha II, Auhea, most familiarly known as the big-mouthed queen. This was a fine building of colored stone plaster with a wide veranda and every convenience suitable for those who occupied it."[152]

The east side of Halekamani was bounded by a bank of Loko o Ho'olili, and Premier Keoni Ana controlled the east half of the fishpond and its adjacent land as his residence. Directly to the south of Keoni Ana's residence, across tiny Loko o Ka'alolo, the premier's sister Fanny Young had a houselot. Across the government road to the east was a houselot of her husband, George Na'ea. The remaining beachfront of Pākalā, just south of Chief Pākī, belonged to Victoria Kamāmalu, daughter of Kekūanāo'a and Kīna'u.

Directly to the east of Na'ea's lot stood the holdings of R. Kalaipaihala, which he received in 1823. A small road formed the northern boundary of this property, and an arm of Loko o Mokuhinia existed to the south. Kalaipaihala was among the largest landowners in Waine'e. Fornander records a Kalaipaihala as having been *punalua* with Kamehameha I's full brother Keli'imaika'i and Kalikolani.[153] The child of the threesome was Ka'ō'ana'ena, John Young's second wife and mother of Fanny, Grace, Keoni Ana, and Gini Lahilahi, and grandmother of Queen Emma. It is quite possible, then, that the Young family holdings in Pākalā were ancestral.

Across the northern extent of Loko o Mokuhinia, the claims of the Hoapili *mā* became dominant; these included the residences of Kaihe'ekai and his cousin, the *konohiki* Pikanele. The latter was a close associate of Hoapili and accompanied him to O'ahu to negotiate with the rebellious Liliha during the uprising of 1830–31.[154] Pikanele was a prominent member of the church with Hoapili, David Malo, and others. To the north of Pikanele's property was small Loko o Puakō, which also extended northward into a certain Mr. Swinton's property. On the northwest, John Crowder received a small house lot in 1839 from Kaheiheimālia for his services as a blacksmith. The *kuleana* of Pākalā are listed in Table 2. Nearly all the awardees are *ali'i*.

On the east of Loko o Mokuhinia lay the settlement of Waine'e 1, another major component of Kalua'ehu. The *ahupua'a* of Waine'e was created Crown Land by Kauikeaouli during the Mahele, but reserving the *kuleana* rights of the *maka'āinana* and lesser chiefs on the property. More properly, the sovereign received the land by the commutation of William Charles Lunalilo and possibly J. A. Kuakini Opio for consideration elsewhere in the kingdom.

Waine'e was a discontinuous *ahupua'a*, with a small beach, *loko wai*, and *lo'i* section (Waine'e 1), followed upcountry by a large *lele* (discontinuous land) of *kula* (dryland fields) and terraced fields (Waine'e-nui or Waine'e 2). As in Pākalā, many of the houselots for each *kuleana* claimant were located toward the beach, and often *lo'i* and *kula* lands were awarded in separate *'āpana* (parcels), sometimes in different *ahupua'a*. In Waine'e, however, the entire beachfront was occupied by the king, and housesites for Waine'e *kuleana* holders were mostly in less prestigious plots far to the east of the beach and *loko*.

Directly to the east of Pikanele's land and south of Catalena's in Waine'e 1 was an *'āpana* of Ualo. This lot was Ualo's ancestral *lo'i* from the time of Kamehameha I and had been placed under the rule of Hoapili (NT 7:17). The houselot

Table 2

Selected *Kuleana* of Pākalā, Lahaina, Maui

LCA[a]	Claimant	Type	Acreage	Acq. from	Date acq.	BCQLT[b]
206	A. Catalina	houselot	0.24	Crowder	1845	1:263
5320	A. Ka'eo	houselot	0.21	Ka'aimalolo	1844	10:542
373	S. La'ahili	houselot	0.28		1826	10:361
277	W. Lunalilo	houselot	0.81	Hoapili	1841	9:701
339	Kalaipaihala	houselot	0.33		1823	2:43
395	Kahikona	houselot	0.84	Kalaipaihala	1847	10:506
484.1	Kaihe'ekai	houselot	0.2	Kekau'ōnohi		2:1325
476	Pikao	houselot	0.07	Na'ea	1847	9:72
8519-B	F. Young	houselot	1.14	John Young, Sr.	1835	10:301
300	A. Pākī	houselot "Panaewa"	1.18	Ka'aimalolo	1837	10:585
10427.2	Na'ea	houselot	0.38	Pikau/Pikao	1846	2:1433
310.3	Pikanele	houselot	1.168	Kalaiwohi		2:1498
10806.77	Kamehameha III	houselot "Halekamani"	0.69	Nāhi'ena'ena	(1836)	10:607

[a] Land Commission Award number.

[b] Board of Commissions to Quiet Land Titles' *Indices* (1929).

of Governor Hoapili formed most of the eastern boundary of Loko o Mokuhinia in the first half of the nineteenth century, in an area known as Kuloloia. Perhaps not coincidental, a similar place name is found at Honolulu. The beach of Kuloloia also was directly east of the king's palace at Pākākā.

Crossing the ancient Pi'ilani government road *mauka* of Hoapili's house was the area known as Waine'e-nui. Evidence of prodigious agricultural activity, Waine'e-nui terraces extended far back into Kaua'ula Valley. This region was far beyond the outer circle of *ali'i* residences surrounding the king, beyond Kalua'ehu. Most of these outer Waine'e lands were awarded as *kuleana* to former *maka'āinana* tenants. Much of the distant *'āina* was used for housesites, *lo'i,* and gardens. Mahele-era land tenure for the Crown Lands of Waine'e is summarized in Table 3.

Just south of Waine'e was the small *ahupua'a* or *'ili* of Waiokama. This was also part of the royal enclave of Kalua'ehu in the 1830s and 1840s. Waiokama is named for Maui king Kamalalawalu, the "waters of Kama." Kamalalawalu was a son of Kihaapi'ilani, thus nephew of Kihawahine. The extant cemetery of Waine'e Church lies within Waiokama, as did the southern third of Loko o Mokuhinia and the southern half of Moku'ula.

During the Mahele, Waiokama was granted to Lota Kamehameha, future King Kamehameha V, less *kuleana* claims. His claim derived from being the heir to Hoapili, the powerful governor who held much of the lands of Waine'e and

Table 3
Kuleana of the Crown, *Ahupua'a* of Waine'e, Lahaina, Maui

LCA	Claimant	Type	Acreage	Acq. from	Date acq.	BCQLT
4878-FF.1	Po'opu'u	houselot	0.61	Olala	1836	9:11
4878-FF.2	"	---	0.15			
4878-FF.3	"	*lo'i*	0.106			
4878-O.2	Olala	houselot, *kula*, taro *mo'o kula*	0.56[a]	---	---	10:103
3425-B.1	Alu	*kula*	1.45	Kekaluna	1833	9:95
782	Birch	houselot	0.35	Hoapili	1839	3:56
241	Burrows	houselot	0.81	Hoapili	1839	1:273
6787.1	Hanaumua	---	1.3[a]	Kalaipaihala	times of Hoapili	9:4
4878-N.1	Kaekae	---	0.075			
4878-N.2	"		0.325	Kane	times of Hoapili	9:227
322	Kaipo	houselot	0.477	Jones	---	9:189
5207-B.1	Kalaipaihala	---	547.5[b]	Kamehameha III	1848	10:508
5207-B2	"		1.59[a]			
5207-B3	"		5.31			
6786	Kamohomoho	---	2.52[a]	Pakawili	times of Hoapili	9:3
6869.2	Kawaioahu	---	c. 0.6	Ualo	9:229	9:64, 229; 10:203
4533.1	Ualo	---	0.528[c]			
4533.2	"		1.0	ancestors	times of Kam I	9:29
4533.3	"		1.375			
9822.2	Ka'ailau	*lo'i?*	0.78	Kalaipaihala	1846	10:139
6785	Kaluahinenui	*kalo, kula, lo'i*	2.1[a]	Kalaipaihala	times of Hoapili	9:5
6463	Kapu	3 *mo'o*, 8 *lo'i*, gourds, taro	0.63[a]	Waihela	1847	10:206
4878-EE.1	Makaiole	5 *lo'i, kula*	2.3	Kahekili (Keeaumoku)	1823, 1824, 1831	10:386
6218.1	Mauae	houselot,	1.13[a]	Waihele(a)	1841	10:41
6218.2		4 *mo'o; kalo*	0.33[a]			
6784	Na'ai	Sec.1- 4 *mo'o* Sec.2- 17 *lo'i*	total 7.64[a]	Kalaipaihala	times of Hoapili	10:225; 9:188, 315
6857.1	Nakaikua'ana		0.26	Hoapili	1839	9:297
6857.2	"		3.33			
9813.1	Namaka	houselot	0.28[d]	Kalaipaihala	1844	9:69; 10:396
9813.2	"	house, *lo'i*	0.14[e]			
9813.3	"		0.95[e]			
9813.4	"		1.075[e]			
9820	Paele	---	0.43[a]	Kalaipaihala	1845	9:138
484	Kaihe'ekai	*kula*	1.69	grandmother	1817	2:1325

[a]Waine'e-nui; [b]Waine'e 1; [c]Kuloloia; [d]Kaua'ula Valley; [e]Waine'e *mauka* of Waine'e 1.

Waiokama as a result of his services to Kamehameha I. It is not known if Lota ever maintained a residence for himself at Waiokama (see p. 87).

Similar to the arrangement of lands in Waine'e to the north, Waiokama commoners lived to the east of the beach and the houselots of the *ali'i*. Beachfront property in Waiokama was occupied by the *konohiki* Kuahu'ula Nalehu. Loko o Nalehu (or Waiokama or Kōlea), a lobe of Loko o Mokuhinia, was his fishpond. He was the son of Kaihanuimoku (*wahine*) and Kāneoa, the latter of Hawai'i chiefly rank.[155] Nalehu, who would become the patriarch of the Shaw family, was the grandson of Hawai'i *ali'i nui* Alapa'inuiakauaua.

Loko o Nalehu at the time of the Mahele was bisected from the north to the south by Front Street. It was also parted east to west by the lands of John Adams Kuakini Opio, the private lots of Queen Kalama (probably an engagement present from Kamehameha III), and the future Shaw Street. The *kuleana* of Timoteo Keaweiwi was a small patch of earth tucked into this watery land. The entire complex of *loko* drained into the Pacific Ocean near this point. Kuakini Opio's house site on the beach at Waiokama was handed down from his father, Chief Waipā, who was a skilled canoe builder for Kamehameha's famous *peleleu* fleet. Eventually the lot became the land of Napaepae, whose name becomes prominent in later Waiokama history.

The intersection of the modern Front and Shaw Streets is very near a small bridge on Front Street that was built over the area where Loko o Mokuhinia drained into Loko o Nalehu. A written reference to this bridge appeared in 1848 in a letter from Keoni Ana to his brother, James Kānehoa, Governor of Maui.[156]

The *kuleana* of Waiokama are summarized in Table 4.

Table 4
Selected *Kuleana* of Waiokama, Lahaina, Maui

LCA	Claimant	Type	Acreage	Acq. from	Date acq.	BCQLT
7715.3	Lota, Kamehameha V	*ahupua'a*	25.86	Hoapili	1848	10:621
312.5	T. Keaweiwi	housesite	0.16	Kukahiko	1836	10:507
10465.1	Nalehu	housesite	0.25	Maele	1839	9:301
10465.2 (etc.)	"	---	0.35			
10644.1	Pi'iko	housesite	0.32	Kanemaikou	1833	10:366
4878.2	Upai	housesite	0.11	Nalehu	1846	2:1330
302	J. A. Kuakini	housesite	0.25	Waipa	1822	10:584
4452	Kalama	---	0.1	Kamehameha III	1836	10:579
14452	"	housesite	0.075			
24452.3	"		0.075			

Wedges, Circles, Sacred Boundaries, and Legal Wrangling

Backing the foregoing discussion of the various components of land in the royal town of Lahaina is abundant documentary evidence of two systems of settlement pattern operating simultaneously during the time that Lahaina was the capital. It is conjectured that the landuse patterns seen by the time of the Great Mahele are artifacts of the imposition of a royal court upon a much simpler settlement structure. This process has probably reoccurred throughout the history of Lahaina.

The older arrangement of lands in the neighborhood of Loko o Mokuhinia is the classic wedge-shaped mountain-to-sea *ahupua'a* system. Waine'e *ahupua'a* once represented a settlement pattern wherein elements of pelagic, litoral, and freshwater fishing resources were joined with terrestrial pondfield and dryland agriculture as well as forest gathering activities to provide diversified subsistence strategies to the inhabitants of the land, most of whom were commoners. The *ahupua'a* was parceled into various *'ili,* each of which probably had several discontiguous segments, or *lele,* located in different resource procurement zones. The *ahupua'a* was managed by a resident *konohiki,* who represented an often absent *ali'i.* A similar pattern may have been found in other Lahaina *ahupua'a.*

It also seems that ancient Kalua'ehu was a land division considerably larger than the tiny, fragmented *ahupua'a* that existed in West Maui by the mid-nineteenth century. The tendency toward greater fragmentation of the traditional *ahupua'a* unit was a characteristic of the years between 1780 and 1850, when more and more levels of chiefs needed to be provided for upon a fixed amount of land. It is possible that old Kalua'ehu was once a traditional, self-sufficient *ahupua'a* that was later divided into Waine'e and Waiokama *ahupua'a.* Perhaps it included Pākalā.

Overlying and superceding the *ahupua'a* system in Lahaina was the concentric political geometry of the royal court. The palace complex at Lahaina, as it existed at its height in the early 1840s, can be envisioned as part of a nested series of circles with the king at the center (Figure 19). Radiating outward from the sovereign in direct proportion to the established sociopolitical distance to him are the residences of his immediate family, his extended family, his ministers and chiefs, and his servants and retainers. The commoners live beyond in increasingly less royal circles. At such a center, a wide-reaching, highly stratified radial system of tribute and taxation replaced a simpler *mauka/makai* orientation of resource procurement and exchange. At such times, no doubt, resident *konohiki* and tenants were dislodged from the better lands of the *ahupua'a* by *ali'i* and royal supporters. Old claims dissolved at the pleasure of the royal will.

The imposition of a concentric royal residence pattern over a traditional *mauka/makai* orientation happened many times in Waine'e, from the days when it

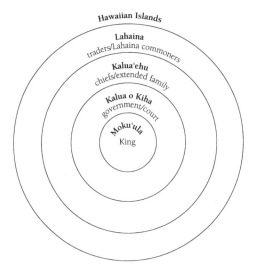

Figure 19. Sociopolitical relationships and the Lahaina landscape.

Hawaiian Islands
Lahaina
traders/Lahaina commoners
Kaluaʻehu
chiefs/extended family
Kalua o Kiha
government/court
Mokuʻula
King

was the primary residence of the West Maui paramounts and the great king Piʻilani to the encampment of Kamehameha I.[157] It happened more permanently during the reign of Kamehameha III. The dissonance between these two traditional systems is seen in the claims and counterclaims for land in Kaluaʻehu which raged throughout the nineteenth century. Even the formality of the Great Mahele could not put some of them to rest.

The control over lands immediately surrounding Mokuʻula itself was a contentious issue in the 1840s and 1850s. In her ambition, it appears that Kekāuluohi forced the hand of her stepfather Hoapili on his death bed in 1840 to ensure that her son, rather than Hoapili's heir, Lota Kamehameha, would receive control over Waineʻe. With Kekāuluohi's own death in 1845, her lands in Lahaina and other regions were passed to son William Charles Lunalilo. In the *Mahele Book,* Lunalilo commuted his interest over the *ahupuaʻa* of Waineʻe for land consideration elsewhere. Only at that point did Waineʻe return to the king. Although all of Lahaina was apparently set aside as private lands by Kamehameha I, *konohiki* for the king had over time usurped the royal prerogative. Waineʻe *ahupuaʻa,* with its sacred royal tomb and residence, ironically did not become Crown Land until it was received back to Kamehameha III by Lunalilo's commutation during the 1848 Mahele. These facts build the case for the wrath of the *moʻo* Kihawahine against Kekāuluohi in 1838.

The king's private lands, known through LCA 10806, and the Crown properties of Mokuʻula, Hale Piula, and Loko o Mokuhinia were surveyed after the Mahele. LCA 10806 *ʻāpana* 77 was the Nāhiʻenaʻena/Gilman property of Halekamani. The Crown Land of Lahaina was surveyed by Monsarrat, probably in the early 1850s, and Mokuʻula specifically so by William Alexander in 1855—but this still did not prevent disputes over ownership even after the death of the king.

What of the lands of Hoapili in Lahaina? This issue is complex and has involved legal proceedings over the years. Yet the documents and oral testimonies relating to disputes over the disposition of these lands have provided perhaps the richest source of survey data on Mokuʻula. For all his adherence to the new ways of the Christian *haole,* Hoapili seems never to have thought of his Waineʻe *ʻāina* as anything other than lands entrusted to him by the *mōʻī* to guard and make productive. In addition to being stepfather of Kauikeaouli, Hoapili was *hānai* father to Lota Kapuāiwa, King Kamehameha V, but there is doubt that he intended to have him as heir as well. Dying in 1840, Hoapili left two written *kauoha* (wills). In 1839 he allegedly wrote:

> Greetings to you, Kauikeaouli, Kamehameha III: Herewith is my thought to you, regarding my lands; to King Kamehameha, to Liholiho, to Kauikeaouli; from Hawaii to Kauai; they are yours, together with lands of Liliha, and the land of Palekaluhi to me, are yours. I have no heir; my heir is dead, my daughter; you know of her death; you are the heir. Your wealth (land) is returning to you, together with the retainers, are yours. Here are your lands; the lands of Kamāhoe [the twins, a reference to his father and uncle, *hānai* sons of Kekaulike], and of Kai [Keōpūolani, his former wife], and of Harieta [Nāhiʻenaʻena, his stepdaughter]; those are your lands; that is all.
>
> By,
>   Uilama Hoapili…X…Who returns them to The King[159]

The lands of Keōpūolani and Nāhiʻenaʻena may well have included Mokuʻula.

Hoapili apparently intended to return his lands to the king. It was traditional at that time to leave the land to the next highest *haku* (lord), and to Hoapili, an *aliʻi nui* himself, that person was Kauikeaouli. Kamehameha III was also his stepson, a *punalua* son through Hoapili's marriage to Keōpūolani, and heir to the property of Nāhiʻenaʻena as an individual.

This particular will was "proved" in a tribunal of *aliʻi* to be the fraudulent work of high *konohiki* Kinimaka, *kahu* to the future King David Kalākaua. Kinimaka was a close associate of ʻAikanaka, King Kalākaua's grandfather and Hoapili's closest biological heir after Liliha. Although it seems likely that he was framed, Kinimaka admitted his forgery and was exiled to Kahoʻolawe for five years. His property was confiscated.[160]

Conveniently, another Hoapili will appeared and was examined by the *kuhina nui* Kekāuluohi just before her stepfather died. It stated that Lota and Kekāuluohi's mother, Kaheiheimālia Hoapiliwahine, were Hoapili's heirs. Learning of this, Kekāuluohi visited Hoapili on his deathbed. Under pressure from Kekāuluohi,

Hoapili denied the earlier will and thus made Lota and Kaheiheimālia his heirs, naturally under the execution of the *kuhina nui* Kekāuluohi.[161] Thus Hoapili's lands passed from the control of the king to that of Kekāuluohi.

Based on this information, the land tenure of the *ahupua'a* of Waine'e was as follows: Kamehameha I most likely placed Waine'e, an ancestral land of Keōpūolani, in trust to Hoapili after the king left Lahaina in 1803. Keōpūolani continued controlling her lands with new husband Hoapili until her death in 1824. Hoapili continued his control over Waine'e until his death in 1840. Instead of reverting to King Kamehameha III, the land was appropriated by Kekāuluohi and blame for the misdeed placed on Kinimaka. Perhaps the *kuhina nui* felt that some of the lands were hers by right from her grandfather Keōua, the former district chief. Regardless of motivation, Hoapili's Waine'e should have passed to Lota Kamehameha at the death of Kekāuluohi in 1845. Instead, it passed to Kekāuluohi's son William Charles Lunalilo, who held it until he was made to commute the property to the Crown during the Mahele. The Mahele trump card brought back Waine'e (less *kuleana*) into the king's possession, where it remained as Crown Land until the overthrow of the monarchy in 1893.

It was general knowledge, after the death of Liliha, that Hoapili's heir was Lota. According to Gilman in the 1840s, "On the mauka side of the water encircling the king's residence [Moku'ula] were the premises of the old chief Hoapili and his wife.... Lot Kamehameha V was his adopted son and heir-apparent to the governor."[162] Lota eventually received the houselot property of Hoapili at Kuloloia, as was surveyed by Richardson in the early 1850s.

Maui Departure

Pressing international matters were convincing the king to move closer to the seat of foreign residence in the Hawaiian Islands, which was Honolulu. In fact, the first half of the 1840s saw matters of supreme importance to the continuation of Hawaiian independence. The county had actually been ceded at gunpoint to Great Britain during the Paulet Affair of 1843. The nation was restored, but not without severely shocking the Hawaiian government and its young monarch. The Lahaina missionary Richards and the king's former chamberlain Ha'alilio were subsequently sent abroad to seek recognition of Hawaiian independence.

The move to O'ahu was not experienced without a certain reticence felt by those who understood the power of Moku'ula and the traditional responsibilities of the king. According to Laura Green and Mary Kawena Pukui, the king was aware of the ancient prophecy of Ka'opulupulu, the *kahuna nui* of O'ahu *mō'ī* Kahahana, who set into motion the chain of events that resulted in the conquest of O'ahu, first by Kahekili and then by Kamehameha. Kamehameha III's own traditional prophet, Lu'aunuialepokapo, remembered the curse of Ka'opulupulu and warned his king, who was the heir to the vanquishers of King Kahahana:

> O chief! this land of Oahu of Lua is made bitter by the fat of the man of god and his words lie like a squirming maggot for Kakuhihewa. If you listen to those who ask that the government to be taken back to Oahu, it will become a maggot which will consume your race. But if you are determined to do this, go pull up the breadfruit planted by the gods at Lei-walo and break the entrance to the fishpond of the gods at Nuuanu on the boundary between the two districts; then your land and your people shall live. And Luakaha shall be your home site.[163]

Stability, international respect, and modernization in land tenure, government, and commerce were the goals of Kamehameha III's rule in the latter years. And the king realized that his time in relative isolation at Moku'ula had to end. But as long as it lasted, life at Moku'ula was enjoyed to its fullest.

The Lahaina palace at Hale Piula was never completed, and the *hale pili* of Moku'ula were never replaced with frame buildings. The legislature met for the final time in Lahaina in 1842, and in early 1845 the royal court moved back to Honolulu. That dusty O'ahu town had become the commercial center of the kingdom, having grown up around the bustling harbor that was the finest in the Islands for accommodating the deep draughts of foreign ships. With what may well be the concluding firsthand account of the royal residence on Moku'ula, Chester Lyman recalls not a miniature of the Prussian court but something still very traditionally Hawaiian: "And not two years ago [1845] a person calling to see the king found his queen standing sentinel at the door of an apartment & was told by her on enquiring that the king was within with the wife of the Premier & it is well known that the king & Premier have their wives pretty much in common."[164]

By now, the economy of the Hawaiian Islands was rapidly monetizing.[165] The early nineteenth century preoccupation with sandalwood harvesting and trade with China and South America was being replaced by the provisioning of whaling ships. The fleet had discovered the cetacean resources of the North Pacific, and Honolulu was the only port in the mid-Pacific. The value of commerce in the kingdom would triple from the 1840s to early 1850. The main business activity in the Hawaiian Islands during this time was not the production of materials but rather trade. The major specialty of this Hawaiian trade was the importation of commodities by foreign ships and their export to settlements in Gold Rush California and Russian America and to the visiting whaling fleets. Most of this trade took place in the port of Honolulu. Although Lahaina was actually visited more by whaling ships from 1837 to 1859, during the peak of the whaling industry, Honolulu was the only port that had facilities to repair ships within a radius of more than 2,000 miles.

The traditional *ali'i* lifestyle practiced at Moku'ula was probably brought to the king's new palace on O'ahu, the original 'Iolani Palace built by Governor Kekūanāo'a for his daughter Victoria Kamāmalu. Getting the governor to give up his splendid residence was an indication of the king's political ascendency.

By the end of 1845, Auhea Miriam Kekāuluohi was dead. In 1846, Keoni Ana (Figure 20) was called upon to succeed to the position previously unattainable by any of Kauikeaouli's close associates; he became *kuhina nui,* a position previously passed on to female heirs of Kamehameha's wife Ka'ahumanu. With the death of Kekāuluohi, the reign of the female *kuhina nui* and the dual system of kingship finally came to an end.[166] Keoni Ana, son of John Young and former Hulumanu, found himself on firm ground where the earlier Kaomi had stumbled. His half-brother James Kānehoa was then invited to assume the governorship of Maui made vacant by Keoni Ana.

The king also kept Keoni Ana's wife Alapa'i at his side as he moved from his residence in Maui to Honolulu. Helping to fulfill his priest's prophecy, prior to moving to O'ahu the king had built a retreat at Luakaha in Nu'uanu Valley above Honolulu (Figure 21). Here he gave adjacent land to Keoni Ana. Keoni Ana's sister Gini Lahilahi and her husband Ka'eo lived directly south of the king's house at Kaniakapupu. Members of the Young family lived next to the king and queen at both the urban enclosure of Pohukaina ('Iolani Palace) and in the deep valley at Luakaha. Both the city palace and the summer retreat on O'ahu were spatial reproductions of the social arrangement codified in the geography of Moku'ula, Kalua o Kiha, and Kalua'ehu in Lahaina.

Figure 20. Keoni Ana, or John Young II, ca. 1850. He was King Kamehameha III's close friend and premier. Bishop Museum CP 103,300.

Figure 21. The king's summer home on Oʻahu, at Luakaha in Nuʻuanu Valley in 1853. Kauikeaouli's love of a private and simple home continued with the move of the capital from Lahaina to Honolulu. Bishop Museum CP 117,635.

The *kuhina nui* court in Honolulu had always been strongly influenced by the missionaries, especially the king's "savior" in the Paulette Affair in 1843, Dr. Gerrit Parmele Judd, and his wife, Laura Fish Judd. The stern Judd was president of the Hawaiian Total Abstinence Union and the Oahu Temperance Society and even convinced the king and queen to stop drinking alcohol for a time. Assuming that the king and queen left to their own devices would eat with their feet, Mrs. Judd arranged for the royal couple to have a "proper" steward and purveyor. Now the king could have a "table spread regularly for breakfast and dinner" rather than his former calabash and finger bowl.[167]

At the palace in Honolulu, the carefree lifestyle of Mokuʻula was replaced with a system of protocol designed by Foreign Minister Robert C. Wyllie to "add dignity" to the person of the king—this in addition to the personal circumspections prescribed by the Judds (Figures 22 and 23). Wyllie believed that a certain Western sense of pomp and circumstance was needed to restrict foreigners' easy access to Kamehameha III.[168] Some foreigners protested the restrictions on access, diminishing the sense of their own importance. Smarting, they protested that the court was aping their own systems of royal etiquette. Nonetheless, the *haole* tabu system protecting the privacy (and access) to the king remained in force until the end of the monarchy.

Figure 22. Queen Kalama in Victorian dress and ringlets, ca. 1850. Bishop Museum CP 114,516.

Figure 23. Kamehameha III. Bishop Museum CP 31703

After the court had moved to Honolulu, Kauikeaouli would return occasionally to Moku'ula. The last royal visit to the complex of Moku'ula was recorded in 1846:

> His Majesty and suite landed at Lahaina on the morning of the 17th. They were received by the new governor [James Kānehoa Young] and the other authorities, under the customary salute from the Fort. His Majesty proceeded to the residence of the Premier [Keoni Ana], where he rested for a short time. He then visited the large Palace now in progress [Hale Piula], and afterwards retired to his former residence at Moku'ula. As usual, he visited the tomb of his sister and two children. On the 18th, His Majesty held a levee, at which upwards of 1300 natives and foreigners attended, to express their respects and congratulations.[169]

The Last Resort

Despite the fact that the royal residential complex at Moku'ula and Hale Piula were built on a site highly significant in Hawaiian history and religion, it cannot be overlooked that much of the architectural landscape established by Kamehameha III was Western rather than Native Hawaiian in style. The structures of Hale Piula and the tomb/residence on Mokuʻula are clearly Western by style and function. So too may be other features at Mokuʻula: Is an island fortress surrounded by water, stone walls, and sentries a Native Hawaiian tradition? Could Kauikeaouli and his chiefly and missionary supporters have been influenced by French chateaux and other royal European building styles? The guards were certainly dressed in the height of European military fashion. Kauikeaouli's frustrations, reactionary behavior, and escapism seem superficially similar to that of King Ludwig II of Bavaria, the builder of such weekend getaways as Schloß Neuschwanstein in the Alps. But Mokuʻula was a very Hawaiian place, and Kauikeaouli was a traditional Hawaiian king. Mokuʻula was an expression of the *kapu* of the last divine Hawaiian king—it was his last resort.

In traditional practice, barriers restricting access to the king were occasionally more symbolic than physical. The *kapu* surrounding the *aliʻi nui,* backed by the pain of death, kept people away. When moving through a populated area, criers would announce the approach of the *aliʻi nui* and the proscriptions thereby invoked. In theory, approach to the king could be blocked simply by the posting of *kapu* sticks, or *pūloʻuloʻu*—tapa-covered balls impaled upon sticks. But in traditional practice it appears that the residences of the *aliʻi nui,* like most sacred Hawaiian spaces, were generally demarcated by physical means as well. In early postcontact times, accounts from Malo and Iʻi describe the king's house as being surrounded by a stockade (*pā*) guarded by *kaikuono,* or sentries.[170] A wooden palisade was the case at Kamehameha I's compound at Pākākā in Honolulu, and a stone wall enclosed the royal residence at Kamakahonu in Kailua-Kona, Hawaiʻi. In ancient times, the royal school at Pālama ("Enclosure of lama wood") on Oʻahu was enclosed—there are many other examples. These walls are known as *paehumu,* the *kapu* enclosures traditionally surrounding a chief's house or *heiau.* Royal Hawaiian burial sites are to this day set apart. The Pohukaina Mound on the grounds of ʻIolani Palace in Honolulu is marked with a *kapu,* even though the remains were removed many years ago. The site of Mokuʻula is similar in this regard.

Even after the so-called downfall of Native Hawaiian religion in 1819, *kapu* sticks alone may have been sufficient to demarcate the precincts of the king to his own people. Still, in contrast to the open accessibility of Hale Piula, the moated, enclosed, and guarded islet of Mokuʻula spoke in no uncertain terms to foreigner and *kanaka maoli* alike that this ground was off limits. A few years later in Honolulu, a Western system of protocol was introduced at court primarily to keep foreigners from impinging upon the space and attentions of the king.

The political geometry of Mokuʻula can be envisioned as a transitional form of social regulation and royal demarcation, located somewhere between the ancient *kapu* system and the full integration of Western systems of spatial protocol. This apparent pattern is not confined to the Lahaina site, however. Somewhat the same situation occurred historically with the development of the city of Honolulu. Here, the royal court of Kamehameha I radiated from the compound of Pākākā Heiau on the beach, erasing 'ili and other markers reflecting more common usage of Nu'uanu *ahupua'a*. The more ancient system was permanently lost with the rapid establishment of Western-style street grids and blocks in the years following the abandonment of Pākākā by both the royal and *kuhina nui* courts for Lahaina and Pohukaina, respectively.

The concept of a moated demarcation of sacred and profane social spaces is nearly universal. From Tenochtitlán to Mont-Saint-Michel to the Imperial Palace in Tokyo, a water barrier functions not only for defense but also as a metaphor for purification. By the construction of such barriers, the landscape was made to replicate the underlying religious and political ideology. The ideology behind the design of Moku'ula may been seen as simultaneously foreign and Native Hawaiian, because the concept of the isolation of an elite by physical and social boundaries is similar around the world.

Chapter 5
Ghost Island

The last years of Kamehameha III's life were filled with great responsibility, and no doubt anxiety, as the kingdom moved further into the acceptance of Western concepts of political control, private property, and land tenure. It had become obvious to many in the kingdom that the whaling industry was a precarious business and that Hawai'i was perhaps overly dependent upon it. So too had the lessons of the rise and fall of the produce export market to California in 1848–49 indicated that the Archipelago needed a sustainable economy based on agricultural production. The rise and fall of whaling and cash crops had acutely impacted Maui in particular. All signs pointed to the development of large plantations, and this required a radical land tenure change providing for the private ownership of land. The Great Mahele was the revolutionary act of the last years of the reign of Kamehameha III which placed a seal on the final breakdown in traditional sociopolitical and economic relationships between the *ali'i nui* and the commoners of the Hawaiian Islands.

At the time of the constitutional reform of the late 1840s and during the Great Mahele, Keoni Ana became the powerful Minister of Interior, executing the monumental land reform of the kingdom that occupied Kamehameha III's final days. And the king, who died from alcoholism, left his people the awesome imprint of the Great Mahele, a constitutional government, and recognition of Hawaiian independence by the world powers.

The Death of Kamehameha III

The passing of King Kamehameha III is recorded by Kamakau.[171] The king's death was preceded by the appearance of a vociferous epidemic of smallpox, another "scrofulous disease" associated with the wrath of the *mo'o*. It ravaged O'ahu and Maui from May to October of 1853. In 1854, Kauikeaouli was fatally ill: "Kamehameha III does his best to kill himself with strong drink, and I really believe a great part of the cause lies in the restless talk and tedious warning of the missionaries, in opposition to the old chieftain's pride."[172] Some modern scholars believe that the king drank to excess because of the guilt he felt in giving land to foreigners in the Great Mahele.[173] Perhaps so, but Kauikeaouli, like his brother Liholiho and many of his Hulumanu, played hard and enjoyed life as the traditional prerogatives of the *ali'i nui*. The king enjoyed spirits nearly all his life, except for a few politically astute demonstrations of temperance.

After adjourning the legislature in 1854, Kauikeaouli retired to Kailua and He'eia on the windward side of O'ahu. Here, under the care of Catholic priests, he seemed to restore some modicum of health. Queen Kalama came to visit him, but at the end of her visit he insisted on escorting her back to Honolulu, where he was again tempted by the social scene. After a dinner party at one of the chief's houses, the king drank heavily. Returning home and feeling flushed, he slept that night out in the open on the grounds of 'Iolani Palace. His breathing became labored and he was carried into Keoni Ana's house on the Richards Street side of the palace grounds by the queen and Keoni Ana. Drs. Rooke and Smith were called for, as nausea and convulsions racked the king. After he slipped into delirium, the monarch was moved to his own private bungalow, Ho'iho'iea. When the royal standard was lowered to half-staff and the cannon sounded, at 11:00 A.M. on 16 December, a heartbroken capital knew the king was dead.

As at the death of his mother Keōpūolani, the entire populace seemed to rise with one voice to bewail the death of the king. Queen Kalama was devastated. Kamehameha III's body lay in state at the palace during a period of heavy rains until 10 January 1855, when the funeral train moved through the streets (Figure 24).

Figure 24. The funeral of King Kamehameha III, 1855. Bishop Museum CP 76826.

The king was not buried at Moku'ula. He was initially interred in the royal crypt built for his brother Liholiho and Queen Kamāmalu in the 'Iolani Palace yard. In 1865 his body was removed and interred at the new Royal Mausoleum at Mauna 'Ala, Nu'uanu, O'ahu. For some monarchial purists in the modern Hawaiian sovereignty movement, hereditary legitimacy ended with the death of Hawai'i's final divine ruler, Kamehameha III. For others, legitimacy is only the acceptance of a rule by those inheriting the accomplishments of the past.

Kauikeaouli was succeeded by a grandson of Kamehameha I, Alexander Liholiho, who had at birth become the adopted son of Kauikeaouli. Prince Alexander ruled as Kamehameha IV. Unlike Kauikeaouli, Alexander Liholiho was born and raised a Christian. Moku'ula and the *mo'o* of Loko o Mokuhinia were not important to him. Queen Emma and Kamehameha IV chose to live apart from the main palace at 'Iolani, in a bungalow on the east side named Ihikapukalani. Being a son of Kīna'u and Kekūanāo'a, who were not hereditary *kapu* chiefs, Kamehameha IV did not have the luster or gravity of his adopted father, who was born a living god. Kamehameha IV was not closely related to the Maui royal family.

Keoni Ana himself was taken away in a flu or cold epidemic in 1857. He left an enduring material legacy to modern Hawaiians— Hānaiakamalama, the Summer Palace in Nu'uanu, O'ahu, given to his niece, Queen Emma.

Queen Dowager Kalama continued to stay at Kīna'u Hale on the grounds of 'Iolani Palace and also maintained a residence next to the palace called Haimoepo (Lover's Rendezvous). There she raised her husband's son Albert and continued to maintain a close relationship with her other adopted son, King Kamehameha IV. She entered into partnership with Charles Coffin Harris and managed a successful plantation and ranch on her extensive lands in Kāne'ohe and Kailua on O'ahu. She died in 1870.[174]

Moku'ula in the 1850s and 1860s

The third meaning of the word Moku'ula, "Ghost Island," comes into prominence after the death of Kauikeaouli in 1854. But not all aspects of the royal residence at Lahaina disappeared when Kamehameha III moved to Honolulu. The still unfinished Hale Piula became the government building for the governors of Maui. Moku'ula was not entirely abandoned, either. The residence on the small island apparently was maintained for the king's use until his death. Kamehameha III also left behind the tomb of his immediate family, *ali'i* who represented his heritage from the old Maui and Hawai'i royal families, in addition to the remains of the last king of Kaua'i. The last known interment was in 1851.

A summary of the burials at the tomb of Moku'ula is provided in Table 5. Other Maui *ali'i* were also probably buried there after the abandonment of the old tomb at Halekamani, but we are lacking documentation. According to the Hen-

Table 5
Probable Burials at Tomb on Moku'ula

Individual	Relationship	Burial	Comments
Hoapili	stepfather of Kamehameha III	1840	father of Liliha
Kaheiheimālia	wife of Hoapili	1842	mother of Kekāuluohi
Kekau'ōnohi	granddaughter of Kamehameha I	1851	1847 date from Henriques genealogy is wrong
Kaumuali'i	husband of Ka'ahumanu	(1824) 1837	last king of Kaua'i
Nāhi'ena'ena	sister of Kamehameha III	1837	died Dec. 1836
child	child of Nāhi'ena'ena	1837	prb. child of Kamehameha III
Keōpūolani	mother of Kamehameha II, III, and Nāhi'ena'ena	(1823) 1837	moved from Halekamani
Liliha	stepsister of Kamehameha III	1839	wife of Boki
Keaweawe'ulaokalani I	son of Kamehemeha III and Kalama	ca.1839	
Keaweawe'ulaokalani II	son of Kamehameha III and Kalama	ca.1842	

riques genealogy, Kekau'ōnohi was buried at Moku'ula six years after the island had been abandoned as the capital residence of Kamehameha III. Moku'ula continued as a mausoleum until around 1884, when the royal remains were reportedly moved to the grounds of Waine'e Church or to O'ahu.

King Kamehameha III's successor, Alexander Liholiho, Kamehameha IV, and his wife Emma rarely visited Lahaina. It appears that the royal residence of Moku'ula was abandoned upon their succession.

Even while Moku'ula was being forgotten, the original tomb of Lahaina and residence of Keōpūolani and Nāhi'ena'ena, the enclosure at Halekamani, was itself a sore point of contention between royal family members. When the princess died in 1836 and the bodies of the Maui ali'i were removed to Moku'ula, Kekau'ōnohi was given charge of the property. After Kekau'ōnohi's death in 1851, ownership of Halekamani was claimed by her widower, Levi Ha'alelea, who contested the claim of this parcel by the king. But the Crown prevailed. In 1855 the Land Commission Award of Halekamani went to Kauikeaouli's heir, Alexander Liholiho.

In the meantime, in 1852, Gorham Gilman, received a lease for Nāhi'ena'ena's Halekamani house from the Crown.[175] The importance of Lahaina as half way between the island of Hawai'i and Honolulu was noted by Gilman, as it "was often a pleasure to entertain guests passing from one island to another," including, apparently, the young Lili'uokalani.[176] His house, apparently, was the center of the social scene.

Gilman wrote to the Interior Department to request that the old tomb of Pā Halekamani be repaired, the ceiling raised three feet to increase value to lease to "transient people."[177] Actually, the old tomb was to become the new site of the U.S. Consul. On 1 April 1859, the Crown leased the Halekamani tomb to George Brayton, U.S. Consul, for five years for $1, provided Brayton performed the needed repairs.[178]

The famous Victorian travel writer Charles Stoddard wrote of his stay in Lahaina and vividly recalls staying in a tomb of the *ali'i*.[179] Although the account is most likely partially fictionalized, Stoddard's description would seem to fit the dark, windowless tomb at Halekamani, perhaps just before Brayton assumed the lease and remodeled it with a *lānai* and partitions within. His description does not seem to fit the descriptions of the sepulcher of Moku'ula, which by all accounts was of two stories and had windows and twin *lānai*. House-hunting, Stoddard seems to have discovered that the only available stone house was the old tomb: "It was an airy mausoleum builded of coral blocks; within it of old were ranged the sarcophagi that encased the spiced dust of the mightiest of their race." Stoddard recalls the days of the entombment of Keōpūolani and Kaumuali'i and the encampment of mourners:

> the tomb was "To Let," nobody seemed to care for it any longer. Once upon a time it had been as the Holy of Holies. Never anyone who was hatted passed near it without uncovering. Not a day went by but there was wailing there....
>
> It was a place of pilgrimage, a shrine to which willing and loyal hearts wended their way from the uttermost parts of the kingdom. It was the season of communion among the gods and no mere mortal ever ventured there in the darkness. No wonder it was "to let"; the finest, airiest, roomiest chamber in the port "for rent" and yet suffered to remain untenanted year after year, and avoided even in daylight by all the passers-by as if it had been a pest house. This unsealed sepulcher I could have for the asking. It had been unvisited for a generation; no one cared to enter and explore it; yet no one would ask to have its walls thrown down.

If the remains had been emptied and moved to Moku'ula after the death of Nāhi'ena'ena in 1837, a full generation would have passed before Stoddard appeared in the late 1850s. The following description also seems to match the plan of Halekamani in the Van Dyke collection: "if its walls were whitened and a window or two let into them it might present a pleasing and even cheerful appearance.... What was needed most was a deep veranda, or *lanai,* before it, and a door opening on the side or rear that would admit one to a sleeping room to be added by the occupant."

Stoddard and his dog spent a night in the tomb and were visited by a ghost dressed in feather helmet and cape. Like the goblins of Bald Mountain, the specter disappeared at the faint toll of a "bell in the tower of the native church at the other end of the village." If this was Waine'e Church, then this tomb could not be that of nearby Moku'ula. On the second night of his stay in the tomb, the phantom appeared again and pointed to flagstones in the corner of the crypt. The next day, Stoddard excavated the floor of the mausoleum. He discovered the bones of a chief, dressed in a rapidly disintegrating feather cloak and helmet. He removed and kept for himself a perfectly preserved *lei niho palaoa,* the whale's tooth insignia of *ali'i* rank.

George Washington Bates, visiting Lahaina in 1854, noted that Hale Piula, more recently used as a courthouse, was not only not completed, it was already falling apart: "In the rear of this ruined pile (Hale Piula) is a large fish pond, in the centre of which, and on a small island, stands a small tomb containing several defunct members of Hawaiian nobility, some of whom wandered over this shore before the face of the first foreigner was seen by any of them."[180] No mention is made of any other structure on Moku'ula.

Also in the 1850s, Laura Fish Judd provided a desolate description of the site: "Opposite to these ruins (Hale Piula), there is a large pond, in the centre of which there is an Island connected with the main land by a narrow strip of ground. A large gate which is kept locked prevents any intrusion to the place. There are several houses and some trees on this Island, the King owns them all."[181] The sentries, once stationed about the grounds and yards, were gone. Perhaps Laura Fish Judd's remarks were made after Hale Piula had been more completely destroyed by powerful Kaua'ula winds in 1858.

Among the last documented references to Moku'ula and its tomb is the rather remarkable account of Sophia Cracroft, who accompanied her aunt, Lady Franklin, on their journey from England to Hawai'i in 1861.[182] They were greeted in Lahaina by old American businessman Gorham Gilman, who walked them through Pākalā and Waine'e:

> We were taken by the agent of the steamer, Mr. Gilman, to his house [Nāhi'ena'ena's], a native grass one of the best class—a fine lofty centre room with a door at each end and rooms opening out on the sides: the whole of grass, except of course the frame-work of slender logs of wood— these are perpendicular to the height of about eight feet the lofty roof falling inwards springing from it, beams intersecting as in a church. The floor was covered with matting, and the furniture American, like the owner.

Amazingly, the grass house had stood for nearly forty years. The party, heading southward, stopped at the nearby house of Fanny Young Na'ea (Figure 25), mother of Queen Emma:

In our walk we came to a native house of the best class (not built of grass) and shaded by magnificent trees. A native lady was seated in an armchair under the deep verandah, who we were told was the Queen's mother. She came down the steps to meet us and shook hands with us, desiring that my Aunt should be told that she apologised for not accompanying her in our walk, on account of having hurt her foot. She was a half-caste native, dressed after the usual fashion, but in better material than the common people.

Cracroft then described the tomb at Moku'ula:

We walked to a stone building within which were the coffins of several members of the Royal Family, encased in crimson velvet, studded with gilt nails and other ornaments, and from there passed, on our way, over a small island surrounded by a mountain streamlet, on which the earlier kings had a residence. The vegetation was luxuriant, and we saw several shrubs bearing a silky cotton bursting out of its pods.

The tomb was still a repository for the remains of the *ali'i* at this late date, but the former royal residences were not mentioned as existing. They were perhaps gone by this time. After visiting Moku'ula, the party apparently crossed the small cause-way to Front Street:

After leaving the place of sepulture, we were met by an open carriage of true Yankee build in its form and lightness, belonging to the American Dr. White, who drove us from one end to the other of this extensive vil-

Figure 25. Fanny Young Naʻea, ca. 1860. Daughter of John Young, Sr., mother of Queen Emma, and resident of Lahaina. Bishop Museum CP 112,644.

lage along a road running parallel with that on the seashore, both of which are lined more or less closely with houses and gardens.

These descriptions match the plan of the area executed around 1860 (Figure 26).

Another late reference to the tomb of Moku'ula is provided by Rufus Anderson, who wrote in 1864: "From my first arrival I had looked forward to a visit to her [Keōpūolani's] burial place, it having been one of my early missionary duties

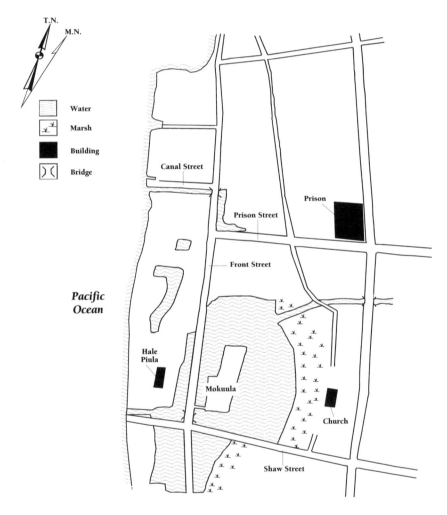

Figure 26. Map of Lahaina, ca. 1860. Redrawing of registered map no. 500, Hawaii State Survey Office.

to edit a small memorial to her. The stone house said to contain her mortal remains is in full view from the protestant church [Waine'e]."[183]

Continuing Debates over Land Tenure

The land tenure conflict in Kalua'ehu that resulted from the superimposition of a *kapu* royal residence on a traditional *ahupua'a* system continued throughout the nineteenth century. It took the courts to straighten out the contested border between Waiokama and Waine'e, between the natives of the land and the great chiefs who had recently settled upon it. The debate over Waiokama in the 1860s and 1870s provides numerous clues to the nature of the former royal enclave of Lahaina and insight into the hereditary guardianship of Kihawahine. The 'ili of Waiokama, lying just south of Moku'ula, was not Crown Land, but it was associated with the caretakers of Loko o Mokuhinia, the hereditary *kahu* of Kihawahine. Lota Kamehameha was the heir to Hoapili, the last high priest of the lizard goddess before the official end of Native Hawaiian religion in 1819.

Although Lota was heir to Hoapili, he was actually given Waiokama by Kauikeaouli in 1848. Kaheiheimālia's will of 1842 had given the responsibility of managing the 'ili of Waiokama not to Lota but to the *ali'i* Nalehu (an ancestor of the Shaw family) under her daughter Kekāuluohi.[184] Thus Kekāuluohi, Nalehu, and Lota and their respective heirs had competing claims to all or parts of Waiokama.

The matter was unresolved in 1872, the year Lota died. The problems of Waine'e and Waiokama, not to mention much of the land tenure of the kingdom, were compounded by the king's intestate departure. The closest natural heir to Lota was his half-sister, Princess Ruth (Ruta) Ke'elikōlani (Figure 27), daughter of O'ahu governor Kekūanāo'a. Ruth came to possess many of the Lahaina lands of Lota. Of immense physical presence, Ruth was the richest woman in Hawai'i in the 1870s and maybe the shrewdest. By outliving her siblings, she inherited most of the massive private lands of the Kamehameha family, lands that had been set aside by Kekūanāo'a for his royal children. Like her uncle Kauikeaouli, she was a traditionalist—perhaps the last chiefess who upheld the dignities of a traditional *ali'i nui*. She reportedly stopped the lava flow of Mauna Loa while governor of Hawai'i.[185] Ruth also claimed the Crown Lands at the death of Lota, and no doubt she would have accepted the crown itself had it been offered to her.

Ruth inherited Waiokama while neighboring Waine'e remained Crown Land. To complicate matters further, before his death the bachelor King Kamehameha V adopted the daughters of Patrick and Lahela Shaw. Patrick Shaw (1830–1907) and his father William Shaw (1807–58) had served as governors of Moloka'i. Lahela Kuahu'ula Nalehu Maelenopuhihiwa Kailiponi Kauhiokapau Shaw

Figure 27. Ruth Keʻelikōlani. A *punalua* descendent from Kamehameha I, she should have become queen at the death of Kamehameha V. Bishop Museum CP 77,396.

(1832–94) was the daughter of Kuahuʻula Nalehu,[186] who received but a small *kuleana* claim in Waiokama. In addition to the land he supposed was left by Kahei-heimālia, Nalehu was to receive "nine gourds, 1 barrel of molasses, and 12 sugar bags."[187] Lahela Shaw finally bought Waiokama from Ruth.

Nalehu would have had a strong claim to Waiokama under the subsequent Mahele proceedings as having been its *konohiki*. He actually received just under four acres in Waiokama. These small parcels were originally given him by Maele in 1839, under the supervision of a Namauʻu. It is possible that Nalehu was removed as *konohiki* under the administration of Kekāuluohi, so by the time of the Mahele the land was under the control of Namauʻu.[188] The award of land to Nalehu in 1839 by Maele may have predated Nalehu's tenure as *konohiki* under Kahei-heimālia.

Legal problems were just beginning for the Shaw family. In the 1850s, Lahela claimed to be the heir of H. Hewahewa.[189] She stated that her father Nalehu was Hewahewa's nephew. A Habakuke Hewahewa had been a major *konohiki* for Kaheiheimālia on Maui,[190] but probably not of the lands of Waiokama. Lahela was denied this claim by the court.

The two daughters of Patrick and Lahela were known in later years as Mrs. Alice Zephr Kaehukae-a-Kamehameha Shaw Kaʻae and Mrs. Mary Kawaiele-apu-ika-lani-a-Kamehameha Shaw Hoapili, but they were named Kaehukae and Kawaiele, respectively, by their *hānai* father, Lota, King Kamehameha V. The Shaw daughters, being true heirs of Kamehameha V, would also be beneficiaries of the

Figure 28. Possible site of Alice Shaw Kaʻae's home, Loko o Nalehu, Waiokama. The waters of Loko o Mokuhinia would be entering from the right. This is probably the site of Queen Kalama's houselot LCA 4452.3. R. J. Baker Collection, Bishop Museum CD 27353.

king's claim to Hoapili's Kuloloia in Waineʻe, and thus to much of the eastern and southern shoreline of Loko o Mokuhinia. They would inherit the claims of their grandfather Nalehu (Figure 28), and most likely the ancient position of *kahu* to Kihawahine.

In 1879 the Shaw family went to court. Part of the Crown Land of Waineʻe previously surveyed by Monsarrat and Alexander and Bishop was claimed to be part of Waiokama under ownership of the Shaw family. The Boundary Commission heard the case. Testimony provided during the deliberations provides some of the most precise detail about the physical dimensions and structures at Mokuʻula at that time and the immediate past.[191] It also reflects the general confusion at the time regarding the status of the Crown Lands versus the private properties of Hoapili, Lota, and the Shaw family.

Lahela Shaw provided the following testimony:

> Lahaina is where I live. I am familiar with the boundaries of the *ahupuaʻa* of Waiokama. Kānemaʻaikoa owned it before, then to Maele, then to Nalehu for Kamehameha [V], and from Kamehameha to [Ruth] Keʻelikolani, and from Keʻelikolani I bought it. I have lived here since my childhood. I am familiar with the boundaries at the time of my father Nalehu.

Halemano surveyed under the directions of the residents and myself. Halemano showed me the picture—this is what was left, this is right and correct. Start at the *hau* tree pit that is left at the corner on the ocean side of Waine'e church. Go along the stone wall and *lo'i* bank, and between, go until you arrive at Moku'ula. Go seaward and at the back of Napaepae's house go until you reach the sea. Napaepae's house is in Waiokama. Go to the sea to 'Ūhā'ilio, alongside the *pā* of Kamoemalie, go inland, alongside Ko'oka, Pua'aiki, Pua'anui, go seaward of the Government Road until Waine'e and return again to that *hau* pit. The church is slightly within Waiokama. Malalaukalo is only a name—it is within the *ahupua'a* of Waiokama.

Lahela's land tenure follows the description of land that was testified by her father Nalehu during the Mahele for the smaller parcels he was actually awarded. Lahela, like her father, claimed occupation of Waiokama as *konohiki*. The Shaws had to purchase it from Princess Ruth, although Lahela was a *hānai* daughter of Kamehameha V.

A Shaw witness named Poholopu stated that the wall next to the church that separates Mokuhinia from the Waiokama section of the church property was built by Pa'ahana. He wanted to wall off the entire Waine'e–Waiokama boundary, but Kamehameha I put a stop to it. Pueo had been *konohiki* during Pa'ahana's efforts, and Poholopu had helped with the wall. Poholopu stated that the springs of Moku'ula belonged to Waine'e, and that Waiokama "is not a Crown Land."

Auwae[192] was a witness for the Crown, and his testimony paints a much larger Waine'e, one that extended perhaps even farther south than Shaw Street:

> I am a native of Lahaina. I was born at Wailuku. I lived here as a small child with Hoapili. I am familiar with the boundaries of Waine'e. Hoapili pointed out the boundaries to me. Here's the boundary between Waine'e and Waiokama: Begin at the ocean, go along the stone wall of Kaleimoku's [Kalaimoku] house until reaching the *hau* tree, from there go straight along the road [Shaw Street] and ascend upland until the wall of Waine'e; at an *'auwai* go straight along the seaward edge of the wall of the church. Waiokama is not within Mokuhinia. It only has a *lo'i* in the front—some of us who were shown the boundaries by Hoapili have died—I am the only one left. I was grown at that time, and married, and afterwards Hoapili died. I am 64 years old now. We all went with Hoapili to show the men of Kalama because Hoapili gave Mokuhinia for Kalama, after Nāhi'ena'ena took Mokuhinia for herself; because of thinking only of herself, Nāhi'ena'ena died, and it fell to Kamehameha [III]. I was not shown the boundaries of Waiokama—I only know the boundaries of Waine'e.

There are two Waine'e, for Waipa and for Kaiokoili. Mokuhinia is in Waine'e, La'ahili cared for Mokuhinia, and afterward Kānema'aikou, and [then] Maele, and afterwards it fell to Keawehano. Hoapili was the only one who showed me the boundaries; the *ali'i* at that time knew the bones of the land, and sometimes the *ali'i* took the land of [other] *ali'i*. I was shown the boundary between Mokuhinia and Waiokama. I was not shown the boundaries around Waiokama. Kauikeaouli was the king at the time.

This testimony supports the early claim of Nāhi'ena'ena for Moku'ula and is unusual for bringing Kauikeaouli's wife, Queen Kalama, into the ownership matrix. Many of the Crown witnesses had lived with the *ali'i*, so naturally their recollections tended to agree with the *ali'i* who were claiming portions of Waiokama for the Crown. According to Napaepae's testimony,

That road [Shaw Street] that goes upland is the boundary between Mokuhinia and Waiokama. Waiokama is not within Mokuhinia. Only the *loko* of Waine'e. I was not truly shown the boundaries, but while I was living with the *ali'i*, that is what I understood. In our childhood, we climbed the coconut trees on both sides of that road that goes upland, but we were upset by Hoapili. We couldn't fetch coconuts on that [Olowalu] side of the road because that coconut grove belonged to Waiokama—and the coconuts on this [Kā'anapali] side of the road were for us.

Other witnesses for the Crown also described boundaries about which they had no firsthand experience. Notably, they all claimed that the present Shaw Street was a boundary (Figure 29). They were probably prompted by others.

It appears on the surface that the *ali'i* seemed particularly grasping and parsimonious in the matter of Waine'e and Waiokama lands.[193] In fact, as can be seen in the reference to Kamehameha I preventing Pa'ahana from enclosing Waiokama, the entire island and lake were being established by the king as a center despite preexisting boundaries and prior sociopolitical relationships.

In its deliberations, the commission noted that *ka po'e kahiko*, the people of old, were not accustomed to the separation of *ahupua'a* through the middle of a *loko*. The Shaw family seemed more familiar with traditional markers, noting landmarks such as the large *pōhaku* along the church wall. The Crown witnesses did not seem to have firsthand knowledge of the boundaries. The commission finally set the *ahupua'a* boundary according to the knowledge of the Shaw claimants rather than the Crown. Moku'ula and Loko o Mokuhinia were split in half—the concentric symmetry of the royal court erased. That judgment is reflected on the S. E. Bishop map of 1884 and official tax maps to the present day.

Figure 29. Shaw Street, looking east, 1910. Loko o Mokuhinia is to the left, Loko o Nalehu to the right. This was considered the boundary between Waine'e and Waiokama by the Crown. Ray Jerome Baker, Bishop Museum CN 34736.

A succession of guardians of Loko o Mokuhinia can be reconstructed based on Mahele and Boundary Commission testimonies. These individuals were *kono-hiki* of the royal fishponds of the Maui *ali'i* at Kalua o Kiha. La'ahili appears to be the first known *kahu,* followed by Kanema'akou, who was succeeded by Maele. When Waiokama was split from Waine'e, Nalehu was the *kahu* of the southern pond and associated lands. Waiokama was subsequently owned by Lota, followed by Ruth and Lahela Shaw. Descendants of the Shaw family are thus both owners and traditional *kahu* of the southern sections. As heirs of Hoapili, they could also be considered the *kahu* of Kihawahine. The northern section of the Loko o Mokuhinia region in Waine'e was guarded by La'ahili, Kanema'akou, and Maele, who was followed by Keawehano. After the commutation of Waine'e by Lunalilo, the region became Crown Land and was administered by agents of the king. This ultimately became County of Maui property. In the spirit of the Great Mahele, the lands of Waine'e and Waiokama should have been granted to the guardians of Loko o Mokuhinia, were it not for the sustaining and precluding interest of the *ali'i,* even after the court had abandoned Kalua'ehu for Honolulu. The political partition of the lands of Waiokama and Waine'e during the Mahele, especially the claims of the Crown, reflects a contemporaneous physical separation of *loko*

Mokuhinia and Waiokama with the establishment of the causeway roads that eventually became Shaw and Front Streets. Most likely, Loko o Mokuhinia was once a single, large fishpond.

The Demise of the Tomb at Mokuʻula

Around 1883, Princess Bernice Pauahi Bishop, no doubt mindful of her status as the last legal heir of the Kamehameha dynasty and feeling the first pangs of her own fatal illness, made preparations for various legacies benefitting her people and her line.[194] Although Bernice is no doubt best recollected for establishing the Kamehameha Schools, she also must be credited with assuring proper remembrance and respect for the bones of her royal Maui and Hawaiʻi ancestors interred at Mokuʻula. Alice Kaʻae, daughter of Lahela and Patrick Shaw, claims to have been witness to the reinterment of the royal relics from Mokuʻula to Waineʻe Church. The stone mausoleum had most likely deteriorated beyond repair, and the remains needed a more fitting curation. According to her story as told to Inez Ashdown, Kaʻae recalled a scene that is remarkably reminiscent of the original interments of Keōpūolani and Nāhiʻenaʻena in Lahaina:

> Before 1893 the Alii used to go to church in their canoes, paddling up the Mokuhinia river and around the little island of Moku Ula. The river and pond reached from Shaw street, which was named for my grandfather, to the Old Canal which is now a road between the court house and the Kamehameha III school. I was about seventeen [1884] when Pauahi Bishop sent for the bodies of the Alii who were in the store house on Moku Ula. That place was kapu to all but high Alii who were noble and did great deeds. The Moo would drown any bad people who broke the kapu and went to Moku Ula. When the wagon and horses came, and the coffins were taken from the building, the people wailed. It was night time, and everyone carried lama (torches), and the coffins were very heavy, for they had sand in them. When everything was ready, the men urged the four horses but they could not move. Then the old people said that the spirits of the Alii were disturbed. Everyone prayed, and some of the oldest ones spoke to the spirits of Alii and told them the moving was the best, for at Wainee and the cemetery on Oahu they could rest in peace. The horses were taken from the wagon and many people pulled the heavy load some distance. Then the horses were harnessed up again, and so the funeral went on to Wainee without further trouble.[195]

Bernice Pauahi Bishop, great-granddaughter of Kings Kamehameha I and Kamehamehanui of Maui, was herself dead by year's end. She was buried in the Kamehameha crypt at the Royal Mausoleum at Mauna ʻAla, Nuʻuanu, Oʻahu. In

1888, Lahela and Patrick Shaw deeded a small portion of Waiokama to the Waineʻe Church to be used as a cemetery.[196] Charles Reed Bishop, Pauahi's widower, erected a monument to Keōpūolani, Nāhiʻenaʻena, Liliha, and other Maui royalty at Waineʻe Church. The monument, having been reconstructed, still stands. Rumors have persisted that the aliʻi remains might not be there, in part because of King Kalākaua, who avidly searched for the bones of Hawaiian royalty during his reign.[197] In 1922, Charlotte Turner wrote: "Keopuolani was in the cemetery near the Waineʻe Church. Some years ago King Kalakaua went through the islands gathering the remains of royalty and placing them in the mausoleum in Honolulu.... Those now living cannot definitely say whether those places in the Waineʻe Cemetery were removed or not."[198]

Much of the ambiguity of the placement of the royal remains is intentional. As with the bones of Kamehameha I, great secrecy accompanies a royal interment, and the care of the remains is under hereditary kahu. In fact, the position of kahu of the royal family has been passed down among the heirs of Hoapili, Kamehameha's kahu, to the present day. The curators of the Royal Mausoleum at Mauna ʻAla today hold that position for the State of Hawaii, no doubt one of the few hereditary civil service positions in the United States.

The Filling of Loko o Mokuhinia

In the late nineteenth century, sugarcane plantations began to dominate the mauka areas above Lahaina. James Campbell of Lahaina and Henry Turton established Pioneer Mill Company in 1865 and eventually covered vast uplands of Lahaina, Launiupoko, Wahikuli, and Kāʻanapali (Figure 30).[199] Some Native Hawaiian families continued to maintain a subsistence culture of fishing and taro production in the area (Figure 31).

Sugar cultivation demands prodigious quantities of water. According to oral recollection, the construction of ditches and reservoirs for canefields above Waineʻe severely disrupted the original flow of water into Loko o Mokuhinia, and the pond became a stagnant swamp. Registered map no. 500 of the 1860s (see Figure 26) shows the fringes of the lake as a marsh.

The change of Loko o Mokuhinia from a lake to a marsh is also portrayed in photographs. Figure 32, the only definitively known photograph of Mokuʻula, shows the cobble-strewn island surrounded by marshland and reeds. This photograph would have been taken around 1894–97. The structure in the background appears to be the ruins of Waineʻe Church, which was severely damaged by a monarchist insurrection in 1894.[200] The alignment of stones in the middle distance may be the remains of one of the holding ponds for the king's fish or bath. Figure 33 was photographed between 1897 and 1914, from roughly the sample

Figure 30. Aerial photograph showing the encroachment of canefields around the tree-lined beachfront of Lahaina, ca. 1930. Bishop Museum CP 99255.

Figure 31. Hale pili of a commoner family in Lahaina, ca. 1890. Bishop Museum CP 112,032.

Figure 32. Loko o Mokuhinia with sedge banks, ca. 1894–97. Moku'ula is in the center ground. Bishop Museum CP 112,019.

angle as Figure 32. Waine'e Church has been rebuilt, but the vegetation and architectural features on Moku'ula are not visible. Reeds are seen to nearly cover the pond. Loko o Mokuhinia is identified as a marsh on the 1914 Sanborn map of Lahaina.

In 1913, businessmen of Lahaina, including Weinseimer of Pioneer Mill and George Freeland of the Pioneer Hotel, initiated a public project of filling in the stagnant waters of Loko o Mokuhinia.[201] It was then popular to fill wetlands in Hawai'i and elsewhere for "hygienic" and developmental reasons (Waikīkī on O'ahu was another example). According to oral informant S. Ichiki, Mokuhinia was filled in 1914 with soil from Honokōwai, north of Lahaina. Ichiki recalls that a temporary rail line, most likely from the nearby mill railroad, was extended to Mokuhinia to bring in the hopper cars of earth. A steam plow was utilized at the site to spread the materials. No documents have surfaced that indicate the origin of the coral rubble also used to fill Mokuhinia, but presumably it is from Lahaina harbor dredging activity. In 1918, Executive Order 52 turned over the newly filled pond for the establishment of Malu'ulu o Lele County Park. On the east side of Loko o Mokuhinia, Hoapili's stone house was still standing as late as 1922.[202]

Crown ownership of this parcel (TMK 2-4-6-7 par 2) was assumed by the Republic of Hawaii in 1893, and then the Territory and State of Hawaii for use by the County of Maui Department of Parks and Recreation. A portion of the site of

Figure 33. Loko o Mokuhinia, ca. 1897–1913. The pond is choked with sedges. Waineʻe Church, in the background, has been rebuilt. R. J. Baker Collection, Bishop Museum CD 27348.

Mokuʻula is presently covered with baseball bleachers. A section of the park, Parcel 41, was conveyed to the Buddhist Hongwanji Mission in 1969 (Executive Order 2447).

Parcel 36 of the modern tax maps contains the Waiokama, or southern, portion of Mokuʻula. Members of the Shaw family lived on the site (Figure 34), which was partially surrounded by remnants of Loko o Mokuhinia as late as the 1970s. The plot had been purchased by Baldwin Packers, then transferred to Maui Land and Pineapple in the 1960s. In 1978 it was conveyed to the State of Hawaii and converted for parks use by the County of Maui by Executive Ordinance 2889. It is presently a parking lot. Parcel 1, the area on the southeastern shoreline of Mokuhinia, was also conveyed from Baldwin Packers through Maui Land and Pineapple to the State of Hawaii in 1976. For many years it was the unofficial Lahaina dump. Overgrown with vegetation, it became a shelter for the homeless during the 1980s.

One of the last remnants of the great Loko o Mokuhinia, Loko o Nalehu (Loko o Waiokama) was filled for the construction of a shopping and hotel complex in the 1970s. Presently, part of Naʻea's old *kuleana* immediately north of Maluʻulu o Lele Park retains some of the swampy character of old Loko o Mokuhinia, as do Parcels 38 and 37 (Salvation Army) south of the park. Wild cotton, mentioned by visitors 150 years ago, still grows around the site, and fresh water still drains onto

Figure 34. Lahaina fishpond, possibly Loko o Mokuhinia, with a southern section of Mokuʻula, ca. 1890. The Shaw family, heirs to King Kamehameha V, lived on a remnant of the island well into the twentieth century. Bishop Museum CP 112,024.

Mākila Beach at the site of the old sluice gate of Loko o Nalehu and Mokuhinia, between the shopping complex at 505 Front and the Lahaina Shores Hotel.

The Future

In many ways, the traditional Hawaiian state ended with the death of Kauikeaouli and the demise of Mokuʻula. The king's successors were born and raised Christians. Although related to Kamehameha I, they did not have claims to the highest blood status in the nation as traditionally recognized. By the mid-nineteenth century, the precious land of the kingdom itself had become a commodity that could be bought and sold. The few Native Hawaiians who had survived that time had become alienated from their lands and disenfranchised from the complex sociopolitical systems that once integrated the chiefs and their people.

On the basis of historical research, the location of the buried site of the royal island of Mokuʻula was predicted within certain portions of Maluʻulu o Lele Park. The estimated location was subsequently confirmed by archaeological excavations and other testing procedures (see Appendix). Not only was the island found to still exist beneath the coral, cinder, and silt fill of the park, but several architectural features, most likely datable to the Kamehameha III period, were found in a good state of preservation. These include a wooden pier, segments of the perimeter retaining wall, and possible building remains. It is possible that much of the island is still preserved under these deposits.

It has long been the dream of many in the Maui community to restore Moku'ula and Loko o Mokuhinia. This dream has at times conflicted with the use of the park for sports activities. In 1995, national attention was aroused when the park's maintenance activities damaged part of Moku'ula's perimeter retaining wall. At that time, Moku'ula was being called "America's most sacred ballpark." There is a long-enduring nostalgia for the glory that was Moku'ula:

"E Ho'i Ka Nani I Moku'ula" (Let the beauty return to Moku'ula)[203]

E ho'i ka nani i Moku'ula, lā	The beauty should return to Moku'ula
I ka uka wale o Waine'e, lā	There in the uplands of Waine'e
Kaua'ula mai ko uka, lā	The Kaua'ula wind is from the mountains
Ka'alani mai ko ke kai, lā	The Ka'alani rain is from the sea
Huli aku ke alo i Lāna'i, lā	The front turns toward Lāna'i
Ma ke kōā iho o Moloka'i, lā	By the lower passage of Moloka'i
Ka malu o ka pu'u 'o Hā'upu, lā	Hā'upu hill deflects it
K'lā pu'u'oni'oni, 'oi kelakela lā	That swaying hill reaching upward
I ka lehua o Kā'ana ke aloha, lā	It is Kā'ana's lehua that is admired
I ka luna wale o Kalae, lā	Only there above Kalae
'O Makakeua ka makani, lā	Makakeua is the wind
I ke kai wale o Mikimiki, lā	Found only at the sea of Mikimiki
Ha'ina ka ino i ka la'i, lā	Tell the refrain about the calm
No Mānoanoa, he inoa, lā	A name song for Mānoanoa

It is appropriate that Moku'ula has been rediscovered during the renaissance of Hawaiian cultural identity and within the modern social movement that is considering the restoration of Hawaiian sovereignty. In the final analysis, the lesson learned by Kamehameha III, Kamehameha I, and earlier Maui kings is a message now being rediscovered: sacred places on the earth persist.

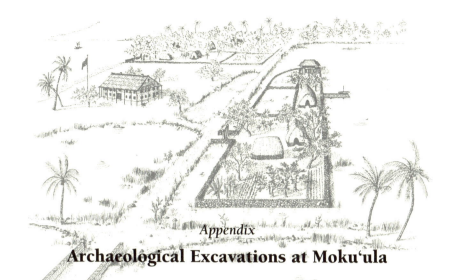

Appendix
Archaeological Excavations at Moku'ula

This story of the island and royal residence of Moku'ula is interpreted primarily through the oral traditions and written records of Native Hawaiian people and their government. In addition, archaeology has provided scientific evidence of minute details of life on the sacred island not previously recorded. An archaeological survey and test excavations were undertaken at Moku'ula in 1993 by scientists from Bishop Museum.[204] This work provided tangible evidence that the island, indeed the fishpond, lies relatively intact under about one meter of coral fill and topsoil.

The main goal of the Bishop Museum archaeological project was to discover Moku'ula's precise location in Malu'ulu o Lele Park. Relatively little archaeology had been done in Lahaina prior to these excavations, and other excavations in the greater park area had yielded inconclusive evidence. Bishop Museum excavations were supported by a grant from the County of Maui, administered locally through the Lahaina Restoration Foundation.

The 1993 archaeological survey was fairly straightforward. To help determine the perimeter of Moku'ula, a series of test pits was excavated by Bishop Museum staff along the predicted borders of the islet. This prediction was made on the basis of preliminary historical and cartographic research. At the bottom of selected excavation units, 14 sediment cores were extracted to provide information on the paleoenvironment of Lahaina and the age of Moku'ula and Loko o Mokuhinia. Finally, a remote sensing procedure known as electromagnetic resistivity was used over the predicted site of Moku'ula to help locate additional subsurface archaeological features and delimit the perimeter. The survey found the remains of the island (Figure 35).

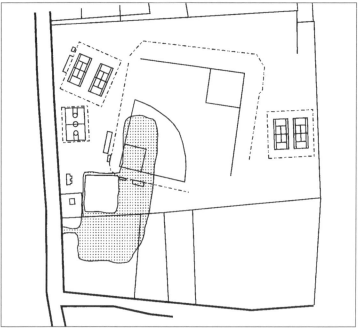

Fig. 35. *Top:* Malu'ulu o Lele Park, Lahaina, 1990. Air Survey Hawaii MA 4-154.
Bottom: archaeological site map, 1993, showing Moku'ula (shaded area).

In contrast to the numerous artificial fishponds found throughout the Hawaiian Islands, archaeological research found that Loko o Mokuhinia is most likely a natural pond, having been in existence for thousands of years. The pond and its island were covered in the twentieth century by at least eight fill components that could be identified throughout the site. The fill has a coral rubble base over which various silt, basalt gravel, and cinder sediments were used to construct the park and baseball field. Beneath these fill layers, the sediment of Moku'ula was identified as a dark reddish brown, silty clay, occasionally exhibiting mottled lenses or layers indicative of dredged pond sediments.

The evidence of Polynesian colonization in the Loko o Mokuhinia area may be among the earliest recorded for the Hawaiian Islands. The precipitation of alluvial material into the pond, determined by core sample analysis, shows gradual accumulation of sediments followed by sediments being deposited at a much greater rate. This fivefold acceleration of alluvial deposition is correlated with the establishment of human habitation of the area. The coincidence of habitation and increased sedimentation may be associated with intensification of cultivation in upland regions of West Maui and Waine'e. Clearing of forests for the establishment of fields for food production may have increased upland erosion and subsequent lowland deposition. The tiny island of Moku'ula is believed to have appeared during this time of initial clearing—an alluvially deposited mud bar abutting the eastern side of the beach swale. The latter feature eventually became Front Street.

The methods used to reach these conclusions were varied and exacting. Pollen samples were examined from pond sediments extracted from a central portion of Loko o Mokuhinia, and some of the organic material recovered was subjected to radiocarbon dating. The pollen analysis and dating were done to identify the first appearance of Polynesian-introduced plants and thus ascertain the date of the first settlement in the area. The procedure was based on general assumptions about pollen accumulation, identification of species, and correlation of those species with human activity.

The abundance of *Pritchardia* pollen in the lowest stratigraphic layer represented in Core 7 (Figure 36) demonstrates that the *loulu* palm was probably more prevalent before the Polynesians arrived than afterward. Perhaps these endemic palms were cut to facilitate agricultural production. The lowest stratigraphic layer in the core that could be completely identified (PIV) contained coconut and taro pollen, indicating Polynesian introductions. The very base of layer PIV was radiocarbon dated at A.D. 45–231. Coconut was most prevalent in the center of the layer, and taro was found toward the top, demonstrating that these particular Polynesian introductions were after A.D. 45–231.

The rate of sedimentation in Loko o Mokuhinia was estimated by radiocarbon dating three samples drawn from Core 7. The resultant calibrated age ranges

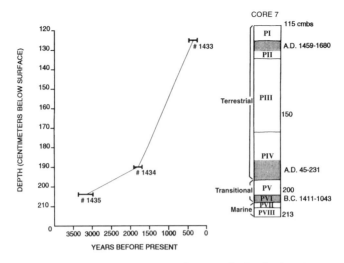

Figure 36. Deposition rates, radiocarbon assays, and stratigraphic levels, Core 7.

were plotted against the thickness of the dated samples from Core 7. Elapsed time between radiocarbon dates was calculated using the midpoint of the three age ranges. A line drawn through the three points roughly reflects the depositional rates of sediments in this section of Loko o Mokuhinia (see Figure 36).

Two deposition rates were found. The rate for the lower section of the core, between radiocarbon samples 1435 and 1434 (containing marine and terrestrial sediments represented in Layers PVI and PV), was 97 years/cm. The upper part of the core, between radiocarbon samples 1434 and 1433 (terrestrial sediments from Layers PIV to PII), was deposited at an apparent rate of 22 years/cm. This is nearly five times faster that the lower rate. Does this indicate a change in the Lahaina environment?

Coconut pollen was first discovered in Core 7 near the midpoint of Layer PIV, about 15 centimeters above the point where radiocarbon sample 1434 was extracted. At the faster rate of deposition (22 years/cm), coconut pollen first appears 165 years after the dated sample, or between A.D. 208 and 393. Indeed, if the appearance of coconut heralds the arrival of Polynesian cultivators, this would represent a very early date for the arrival of Polynesians in Hawai'i in the most widely accepted chronology, and by far the earliest date for human habitation in Lahaina.

As tempting as this tentative conclusion is, a single radiocarbon date and a few grains of pollen cannot provide a statistically valid sample, nor can one presume that sedimentation in Loko o Mokuhinia occurred at a regular rate. Further tests are needed to determine the rates of sedimentation within specific layers of the cores. Allowances must be made for differences in sediment particle size, marine versus terrestrial origin of the sediments, compression factors, and other variables. But it was established that the pollen in the Mokuhinia cores is well preserved. The research establishes interesting questions to guide further pollen research and radiocarbon dating at Moku'ula. If the data can be replicated through further work, the settlements around Kalua o Kiha may indeed be among Hawai'i's earliest.

The pollen record indicates the continuous presence of coconut through the assumed period of human occupation along the shoreline of Loko o Mokuhinia. Ti (kī) pollen was noted in the earliest occupied layer—Layer PIV. *Hau,* an endemic Hawaiian plant used for cordage, was noted in Layer PIII. The record for taro, the staple of the Hawaiian diet, was not consistent through time; perhaps this represents a cycle of taro cultivation followed by periods of inactivity. Above Layer PII, dated to A.D. 1459–1680, there was no evidence of taro pollen in the pond. This may indicate disruption of agricultural activity at the site, but more likely taro was harvested before it flowered and produced pollen.

On the basis of data from all the sediment cores and excavations at Mokuhinia in 1993, the main, artifact-bearing layers of sediment on Moku'ula were formed after A.D. 1459–1680. It seems that this alluvial deposit, slowly creating the small island, began to develop a soil horizon for a time. The deposit of silty material on the western side of the pond, located against the beach swale, appears to have naturally accreted to the east. The process of alluvial deposition could have accelerated in the late eighteenth to early nineteenth centuries. The historical record states that interisland warfare destroyed upland water diversion structures in Lahaina during this time. General forest depletion caused by extensive agricultural clearing, animal husbandry, and forest harvesting would also have tended to increase alluvial or aeolian (wind-blown) deposition into Loko o Mokuhinia. Exploitation of the upland forest continued during the period of sandalwood cutting and ship provisioning in the early to mid-nineteenth century. These factors may account for the emergence of Moku'ula from the waters of Loko o Mokuhinia.

Despite the difficulty in interpreting the pollen analysis, historical documents indicate that parts of Loko o Mokuhinia were used for taro production well into the nineteenth century, and a region on or near the accreting mud bar possessed freshwater springs. Moku'ula, the unmodified land developing to the east of the Hale Piula area beach berm, may have been a place of occasional residence from the late precontact (A.D. 1600–1778) period to the documented establishment of the royal residence of Kamehameha III's immediate family in the late 1820s.

It appears that a substantial portion of Moku'ula was artificially created by dumping pond sediments and possibly other material around a natural silt bar.

Sediments were probably built up on the inside of a encircling stone retaining wall cut into the mud bar. Although we know that the chiefess Wahine Pi'o died on Moku'ula in 1826, the bulk of documentary evidence points to the compound having been built for Princess Nāhi'ena'ena and later her brother Kamehameha III and his immediate family. Based on detailed stratigraphic analysis, it is postulated that pond sediments were dredged from the region off the west side of Moku'ula and placed over the eastern limits of the islet. This activity would have developed a water barrier between the Front Street beach berm and the island, helping to create the moated sanctuary. The dredged area in the pond was then thinly paved with waterworn stones and enclosed, perhaps to provide shallow, clean holding ponds for fish cultivation, drinking water storage, or bathing purposes. By dredging the area to the west and filling Moku'ula, the land would have been built up from about 0.35–0.70 meters above the level of the pond to about 0.70–1.20 meters above that surface. This would be useful for a residence in times of flood and heavy rains. A rampart was then constructed around the resultant island to retain the new sediments. The wall was built in a "cut and fill" method common in traditional Hawaiian wall and terrace construction.

The discovery of substantially more artifactual and midden materials in the northern and central sections of Moku'ula provides evidence for placing the royal residence in this region and supports the spatial patterning of Moku'ula reconstructed from visitors' accounts and other documentation. Even so, only twelve basalt artifacts were recovered during the 1993 inventory survey at Moku'ula within island sediment proveniences: one hammerstone, three edge-altered flakes, six flakes, and two pieces of lithic shatter. This meager assemblage suggests that basalt tool manufacture was not a primary activity on the island. Eight pieces of volcanic glass were found at Moku'ula, including flakes, shatter, cores, and cinders. Like the basalt materials, the relatively poor quality of this raw material suggests that it was probably obtained expediently from locally available sources rather than through importation.

A single example of a one-piece, notched fishhook fragment was discovered in lower island sediments. The object, which exhibits a mother-of-pearl nacre, is carved most likely from *Pinctada* or *Pteria* shell. The small size of the hook suggests fishing activity within Loko o Mokuhinia or at the ocean shoreline.

One sea urchin spine abrader was found in association with Moku'ula. The spine is from the species *Heterocentrotus mammillatus*. It is modified to form a pointed distal end, suggesting its use as a drill rather than a file abrader.

Although chert (flint) is not generally considered indigenous to Hawai'i, it was often used in a traditional manner as lithic raw material for a time after its introduction by Westerners. According to some researchers, flints reflect chiefly and male-associated trade; their presence at Moku'ula may relate to the royal residence. One chert flake, two nodules, and a possible gun flint were found.

The negative evidence of abundant traditional artifacts at the site may simply be a function of small sample size. The lack of traditional artifacts may, however, be reflective of the obsolescence of traditional lithic and other indigenous tool technologies by the time of Kamehameha III's residence on the island. Moku'ula also shows almost no evidence of Native Hawaiian adaptations of Euroamerican or Asian materials (metal fishhooks, edge-altered glass, etc.). In fact, relatively few diagnostically useful nonindigenous artifacts of any kind were recovered from Moku'ula. Those that were identified are generally similar to those found at other pre-1850s sites in Hawai'i.

Most of the nontraditional artifacts that date to the time of Kamehameha III are British earthenwares. The earliest of these are a single edge-decorated pearlware sherd (ca. 1780–1840), dark blue transfer print sherds, undecorated whiteware sherds (probably pearlware or transitional whitewares, ca. 1820–1870), and hand-painted sherds probably predating the Lokelani pattern. Almost all these sherds were found in the area believed to be close to the private residences on Moku'ula.

Five sherds of Chinese stoneware and a single German mineral water bottle sherd were also found during excavations at Moku'ula. Seventeen sherds of Asian porcelain were collected, most from Japanese rice bowls commonly made during the late nineteenth and early twentieth centuries. Rice bowl sherds were also found in a stratum representing an occupation of Moku'ula after the mid-nineteenth-century royal residence had been discontinued. The period of royal residence is most likely not represented in the bottle glass assemblage.

Two brass boat nails were found in island sediments. Their use in Hawai'i is generally dated before 1820. Fragments of machine-cut nails probably fabricated between 1850 and 1900 were also recovered. Considering that date and their location on the far north of the island, the nails may have been associated with the tomb/residence complex of the king. Two shell buttons and one of porcelain were found at Moku'ula, as were glass marbles, lamp glass, beads, table and window glass, electrical cord, concrete, rubber, leather, flower pot fragments, limestone marble, and plastics. These were found mostly in upper fill deposits, however, and are probably not associated with the period of royal residence.

Despite the complexity of the stratification of sediments at Moku'ula and various disturbed contexts, certain patterns may be seen in the assemblage of non-indigenous or imported artifacts. First, there appears to be little hybridization in the transition between indigenous manufacture and traditional use to nonindigenous, nontraditional use. The traditional Native Hawaiian artifacts were found within the same contexts as early imported Western artifacts. With the exception of chert flakes, imported materials do not seem to have been modified for use in traditional ways. These factors suggest that traditional technologies were being utilized simultaneously and discretely alongside imported materials and technologies. Nails were used as nails and not modified as fishhooks.

The relative dearth of materials from the period of royal residence is especially intriguing. Nothing in the assemblage of traditional and Euroamerican artifacts found at Moku'ula, by quantity, style, or quality, demonstrates exclusive royal use. The same could be said of the site's midden (food refuse) remains. This may be due to small sample size or methods of collection, or it could imply that the traditionally meticulous care for the proper disposal of royal refuse was still being maintained during the times of Kamehameha III.

In Hawaiian precontact archaeology, the number of lithic artifacts is often assumed to be an indication of population density, absence or presence of human activity, and length of site inhabitation. This model is, however, usually predicated on the subsistence technology of the overwhelming majority of precontact Native Hawaiian people, the *maka'āinana,* or commoners. Moku'ula is anything but common or even precontact. What should we expect from a royal enclosure in the postcontact era? This is a question presently of great interest to Hawaiian archaeology and history.

Would one expect to find much tool making—such as adze reduction, woodworking, or even fishing—on sacred royal property in precontact times? Sometimes these activities become strictly symbolic among the ruling classes. Manchu emperors ruling from Beijing, for example, led summertime royal hunts in their homelands as a survival from their days as tribal leaders; to this day popes "rough it" by performing marriage rites for common parishioners. Kings Kamehameha I and III were fond of working in the *lo'i* as a way of showing their people the benefits of industry. Other royal sites in Hawai'i that have been partially excavated, like the Ka'ahumanu/Kamehameha I residential complex in Honolulu and the compound at Kaunolu on the island of Lāna'i, reveal extensive household clusters, rich middens, and well-represented assemblages of tools and other artifacts. In general, however, the usual activities of a Hawaiian monarch are not the same as those of the people. The artifacts generated from these royal activities should therefore leave different patterns that are recognizable in the archaeological record. As yet, however, methods of archaeological interpretation in Hawai'i preclude clear recognition of relative social status on the basis of artifact assemblage alone. Usually monumentality of architecture is used as the primary index of social standing at Hawaiian archaeological sites: the bigger the housesite or temple, the more important the personages or activity is believed to have been. At Moku'ula, however, the small size and understated architecture of the sacred royal complex belie that general assumption.

One would expect a king, even a poor king such as Kamehameha III, to have the means to generate considerable refuse. It is highly possible that the lack of artifacts and midden discovered at Moku'ula is simply a matter of small sample size and focus. But such negative evidence may nevertheless be powerfully suggestive; it is quite plausible that the dearth of traditional artifacts at Moku'ula is consistent with its elite residential status. Most likely agricultural products were grown elsewhere and domestic animals tended beyond the small royal enclosure. Food was probably prepared off-site and brought to the island by servants. According to royal Hawaiian custom, food remains and other refuse were carefully collected and disposed of in secret away from the king's residence. All these measures would tend to limit the accumulation of artifacts and midden at Moku'ula.

The inherent *mana* of the *ali'i* and their material culture is at the heart of the matter at Kalua'ehu. In traditional Hawaiian ideology, the personal possessions *(waiwai)* of the *ali'i nui* were charged with nearly the same *mana* as the body of their owner, especially those objects that came into direct contact with that owner. *Ali'i* possessions were carefully guarded by *kahu,* lest their power inflict harm among the common people. When these personal objects were no longer useful, they were often burned or secreted away. Far from being discontinued at the so-called abolition of Hawaiian religion in 1819, the tradition of the sacredness of objects, the association of contagious *mana* with the possessions of the *ali'i nui* continued. Kauikeaouli was born an *ali'i akua* with the highest *mana;* his servants would have been sufficiently traditional to ensure that his personal possessions were well disposed of when no longer needed. This activity may be represented by the relative scarcity of personal objects from the 1837–45 period uncovered through excavations at Moku'ula. Such a practice would also have implications for the analysis of food remains found on the sacred island.

With the exception of worked chert, no nonindigenous artifacts were found at Moku'ula that in any way show signs of being redesigned for other purposes. In many early postcontact *maka'āinana* sites, bottle glass, iron nails, and other Western items were recycled and reapplied to different functions. Again, this seems to be consistent with a postcontact royal Hawaiian establishment. In general, indigenous elites around the world tend to imitate the exotic behaviors associated with the imported material culture—non-elites tend to subvert and appropriate foreign items in subtle and often ironic ways.[205]

Like the issues of sedimentation rate and pollen distribution in Loko o Mokuhinia, the paucity of artifacts at Moku'ula and their form and function generate intriguing questions that remain for future archaeologists at the site. Archaeological work at Moku'ula basically proved the existence of the island beneath modern ballpark fill. The retaining wall that encircled the island was rediscovered. The pavement lining of the spring-fed bathing ponds was located. Postmolds were found, most likely evidence of traditional thatched structures. A large piece of faced basalt was encountered in a shovel probe over the filled pond near the northern extreme of Moku'ula; its position and finish indicate that it could be from the royal tomb. Food remains were found at the site, including many types of fish as well as molluscs, sheep, cattle, and pig. These remains represent both traditional Native Hawaiian and nontraditional resources and food preparation techniques. Several articulated piglets were uncovered in Moku'ula sediments, indicating that they were buried rather than consumed. Perhaps this represents an offering. Human remains representing no more than three individuals were also found at Moku'ula during the excavations.[206]

One of the most exciting features revealed at Moku'ula is a buried pier that extended from the east shore of the island into Loko o Mokuhinia. At about 60 centimeters below the present-day ball park surface, a group of eight wooden planks was found, fastened to a large perpendicular wooden beam by square-headed iron spikes. Beneath this structure was an open space filled with water. It is known that members of the royal family were canoed across the lake on their way to Waine'e Church. The pier was found to be in a remarkable state of preservation (Figure 37). The wood of the pier was identified as Douglas fir (*Pseudotsuga menziesii),* a species exported to Hawai'i as lumber.

Archaeological survey and test excavations showed that Moku'ula was real, and that remnants of it still exist buried beneath a ball park.

Figure 37. Views of Moku'ula pier structure. *Left:* wooden planks exposed in foreground. *Right:* close-up of wooden planks near west end of structure.

Notes

Chapter 1

1. Mary Kawena Pukui and Samuel H. Elbert, *Hawaiian Dictionary* (University of Hawaii Press, Honolulu, 1986), 252. Unless otherwise indicated, all translations of Hawaiian terms in this book are from the *Hawaiian Dictionary* or from Mary Kawena Pukui, Samuel H. Elbert, and Esther Mookini, *Place Names of Hawaii,* 2d ed. (University of Hawaii Press, Honolulu, 1974).

2. See, e.g., Moses Manu, *Ka Nupepa Kuokoa,* 19 January 1884, 25 March 1885.

3. This book is an analysis of Mokuʻula and especially the life of Kamehameha III according to ethnohistorical and historical materials. Appended is a summary of the archaeological findings from Bishop Museum excavations in 1993. These findings are presented fully in P. Christiaan Klieger, ed., Mokuʻula: History and Archaeological Excavations at the Private Palace of King Kamehameha III in Lahaina (Bishop Museum Anthropology Department, Honolulu, 1995).

Chapter 2

4. See, e.g., Kawena Rubellite Johnson, *Kumulipo: Hawaiian Myth of Creation,* Vol. 1 (Topgallant Press, Honolulu, 1981).

5. Abraham Fornander, *An Account of the Polynesian Race* (Tuttle, Rutland, Vt., 1969), 1:190–193.

6. Tone-Iahuan-Tahurlo-Iararie, cited in Elspeth P. Sterling and Catherine C. Summers, *Sites of Oahu* (Bishop Museum Press, Honolulu, 1978), 300. Martha Beckwith, *Hawaiian Mythology* (University of Hawaii Press, Honolulu, 1970), 78. Fornander, *Polynesian Race,* 2:82. Ross Cordy, *A Study of Prehistoric Social Change: The Development of Complex Societies in the Hawaiian Islands* (Academic Press, New York, 1981).

7. Fornander, *Polynesian Race,* 2:87. Samuel Kamakau, *Tales and Traditions of the People of Old* (Bishop Museum Press, Honolulu, 1991), 49.

8. Samuel Kamakau, *Ruling Chiefs of Hawaii* (Kamehameha Schools Press, Honolulu, 1992), 22.

9. Inez Ashdown, miscellaneous letters and notes submitted to County of Maui Planning Department, 1975, Ms. on file, Anthropology Department, Bishop Museum, Honolulu, 1975. Kihawahine's brother Kihaapiʻilani, according to Kamakau, was born at a birthing rock also named ʻĀpuakēhau, at Waikīkī Beach on Oʻahu; see Kamakau, *Tales,* 50.

10. Abraham Fornander, *Fornander Collection of Hawaiian Antiquities and Folk-lore* (Bishop Museum Press, Honolulu, 1916–17), 4:242, 5:176.

11. Fornander, *Collection,* 4:236, 5:164, 166. Beckwith, *Mythology,* 339.

12. According to Samuel Kamakau, *Ka Poʻe Kahiko: The People of Old* (Bishop Museum Press, Honolulu, 1991), 85, the chiefess Kihawahine was transformed into a *moʻo* named Kalamainuʻu.

13. Z. Kepelino, Kepelino's Hawaiian Collection: His Hooiliili Hawaii, Pepa I [1858], *Hawaiian Journal of History,* 1977, 11:39–68.

14. Kamakau, *Ka Poʻe Kahiko,* 54.

15. The two deities fought over a man. Kihawahine was always jealous of her favorite men and was especially fond of those men exhibiting human weakness.

16. John Papa Ii, *Fragments of Hawaiian History* (Bishop Museum Press, Honolulu, 1959), 44–45. Having lived in the household of King Kamehameha I, 'I'i had a uniquely valuable perspective on the structure and function of the royal court.

17. Kamakau, *Ka Po'e Kahiko*, 59–60.

18. Manu, *Kuokoa*, 19 January 1884, 25 March 1885.

19. Kamakau, *Ka Po'e Kahiko*, 82.

20. Beckwith, *Mythology*, 126.

21. Wendell Clark Bennett, *The Archaeology of Kauai* (Bishop Museum Press, Honolulu, 1931), 153–154.

22. P. Christiaan Klieger, *Nā Maka o Hālawa* (Bishop Museum Press, Honolulu, 1995), 11–13, 67.

23. The following review of religious architecture and ritual is from Kamakau, *Ka Po'e Kahiko*, 85–87.

24. Charlotte Turner, Tombs of Ali'i, *The Friend*, December 1969.

25. See, e.g., E. S. C. Handy and E. G. Handy, *Native Planters in Old Hawaii: Their Life, Lore, and Environment* (Bishop Museum Press, Honolulu, 1972), 48.

26. Genealogy Books, Hawaii State Archives, misc. dates, 14:27; 33:44, 49.

27. See William Davenport, *Pi'o: An Enquiry into the Marriage of Brothers and Sisters and Other Close Relatives in Old Hawaii* (University Press of America, Lanham, Mass., 1994).

28. Nī'aupi'o an extremely high *kapu* status, created by the union of half-siblings. Only a *pi'o* child would have higher status.

29. Kamakau, *Ruling Chiefs*, 73–74.

30. On Kahekili II, see Kamakau, *Ruling Chiefs*, 165–167.

31. Fornander, *Polynesian Race*, 2:212–213.

32. David Malo, *Hawaiian Antiquities* (Bishop Museum Press, Honolulu, 1951 [1898]), 56–57. Malo was an early Native Hawaiian schoolteacher in Lahaina.

33. Pukui, cited in Sterling and Summers, *Sites of Oahu*, 26.

34. Kamakau, *Ka Po'e Kahiko*, 85.

35. Kamakau, *Ruling Chiefs*, 259.

36. Cited in Cummins Speakman, *Mowee: An Informal History of the Hawaiian Islands* (Peabody Museum, Salem, Mass., 1978), 72–73.

37. "The power of the female line is an aspect of the myth of the usurper who is tamed by the 'good native' through marriage to an ancient family"; Margaret L. Berman, Towards a Cultural Architecture: Inquiring into Hawaiian Architecture prior to 1778 (M.A. thesis, University of Washington, 1994), 69.

38. Kamakau, *Ruling Chiefs*, 149.

39. George Vancouver, *A Voyage of Discovery to the North Pacific Ocean and Round the World (1790–95)*, Vol. 3 (Hakluyt Society, London, 1984 [1793]), 876. The earliest Western written reports of Lahaina used in this report were penned by explorers such as Vancouver, James Macrae, Louis Claude de Freycinet, Jacques Arago, and later Chester Lyman and Charles Wilkes. In general, their emphasis was on the collection of navigational and natural history data on the Hawaiian Islands. Often these expeditions were motivated by political and economic motives of Western nations during the days of empire. As scientists, their ethnographic descriptions of

Native Hawaiian (*kanaka maoli*) culture at the time tended to look upon indigenous inhabitants as part of the landscape—"Noble Savages" to be appeased or cajoled for the benefit of the expedition.

40. Archibald Menzies, *Hawaii Nei 128 Years Ago* (New Freedom Books, Honolulu, 1920), 105–112.

41. Fornander, *Polynesian Race,* 2:343–344.

42. Kamakau, *Ruling Chiefs,* 280.

43. Kamakau, *Ruling Chiefs,* 260.

44. Kamakau, *Ruling Chiefs,* 260.

45. Speakman, *Mowee,* 96.

46. Kamakau, *Ruling Chiefs,* 189.

47. Speakman, *Mowee,* 97. Some of these causeways, or *kuapā,* eventually became Lahaina streets.

48. P. Christiaan Klieger, Historical Background, in Susan A. Lebo, ed., Native Hawaiian and Euro-American Culture Change in Early Honolulu (Bishop Museum Anthropology Department, Honolulu, 1996), 13.

49. Gideon La'anui, Reminiscences of Gideon Laanui, *Thrum's Hawaiian Annual for 1930,* 89–91.

50. Ii, *Fragments,* 106. Dorothy Barrère, *Kamehameha in Kona: Two Documentary Studies* (Bishop Museum, Honolulu, 1975), 23. cf. Kamehameha Kapuāiwa in Kamakau, *Ka Po'e Kahiko,* 83.

51. Part of the oral tradition, transmitted to me by Dorothy Barrère in 1994.

52. Kamakau, *Ruling Chiefs,* 206.

53. Kamakau, *Ruling Chiefs,* 264.

54. Kamakau, *Ruling Chiefs,* 211–215.

Chapter 3

55. Kamakau, *Ruling Chiefs,* 224.

56. Ralph Kuykendall, *The Hawaiian Kingdom,* Vol. 1 (University of Hawaii Press, Honolulu, 1938), 100.

57. C. S. Stewart, *Journal of a Residence in the Sandwich Islands during the years 1823, 1824, and 1825* (University of Hawaii Press, Honolulu, 1970 [1830]), 33. Many of the primary references to life in Lahaina in the early nineteenth century were written by Congregationalist missionaries from Boston. The works of Stewart, Hiram Bingham, William Richards, and various other authors of missionary letters provide substantial firsthand accounts of the period and are remarkable for their detail. Richards's writings are tinged with a burdensome tone, perhaps resulting from his feeling personally responsible for the education of the children of Kamehameha I and influenced by his position as chief Christian counselor to the royal court in Maui. Stewart's accounts seem more objective, perhaps because his stake in the mission was far more transitory. Missionary wife Laura Fish Judd, although very proud to teach Hawaiians "proper manners," was an excellent observer of human behavior.

58. Cited in Kuykendall, *Hawaiian Kingdom,* 73.

59. *Hawaii in 1819: A Narrative Account by Louis Claude De Saulses de Freycinet,* Ella L. Wiswell, translator, notes and comments by Marion Kelly (Department of Anthropology, Bishop Museum, Honolulu, 1978).

60. Stewart, *Journal*, 177, 182.

61. Stewart, *Journal*, 178.

62. Kamakau, *Ruling Chiefs*, 262.

63. Jacques Arago, *Narrative of a Voyage round the World, in the* Uranie *and* Physicienne *Corvettes* (Treuttel and Wurtz, London, 1823), 2:119–120.

64. Keōpūolani as quoted in Hiram Bingham, *A Residence of Twenty-one Years in the Sandwich Islands* (Hezekiah Huntington, Hartford, Conn., 1849), 195. Stewart, *Journal*, 223.

65. Peter Buck (Te Rangi Hiroa), *Arts and Crafts of Hawaii* (Bishop Museum Press, Honolulu, 1957), 567.

66. Stewart, *Journal*, 226, 230.

67. Bingham, *Residence*, 197.

68. W. Richards and C. Stewart, Letter to *Missionary Herald* (American Board of Commissions for Foreign Missions, Boston), April 1825.

69. W. Richards, Missionary Letters, 1826, 2:746a, Hawaiian Missionary Children's Society, Honolulu.

70. Stewart, *Journal*, 227.

71. Richards, Missionary Letters, 42:746a.

72. Thomas Thrum, *Hawaiian Almanac and Annual for 1928*, 41.

73. Kamakau, *Ruling Chiefs*, 262–263.

74. Stewart, *Journal*, 217.

75. Richards and Stewart, Letter to *Missionary Herald*.

76. James Macrae, *With Lord Byron at the Sandwich Islands in 1825* (Petroglyph Press, Hilo, 1972 [1825]), 11–12.

77. Richard Bloxam, Diary entry, 5 May 1825, Hawaiian Missionary Children's Society, Honolulu.

78. Mitsuo Uyehara, *The Prophetic Vision of Keopuolani, the Sacred Queen of Hawaii* (Native Hawaiian Land Trust Task Force, Honolulu, 1982), 6–7.

79. Kamakau, *Ruling Chiefs*, 265–267.

80. William Ellis, cited in Stewart, *Journal*, 293.

81. Kamakau, *Ruling Chiefs*, 266.

82. Kamakau, *Ruling Chiefs*, 255–256.

83. Speakman, *Mowee*, 88.

84. Kamakau, Ruling Chiefs, 257. Stewart, *Journal*, 338–339, 350.

85. Also a queen dowager of Kamehameha. She was a sister to Kaʻahumanu.

86. Kamakau, *Ruling Chiefs*, 274.

87. W. Richards to Evarts, Letter, 10 June 1826, 2:711–712, Hawaiian Missionary Children's Society, Honolulu.

88. Fornander, *Polynesian Race*, 2:261.

89. Richards, Missionary Letters, 2:746a.

90. Richards to Evarts, Letter, n.d., 2:737a, and Chamberlain to Evarts, Letter, n.d. (1830s), 2:247, Hawaiian Missionary Children's Society, Honolulu. Fornander, *Polynesian Race,* 2:320.

91. C. S. Stewart, *A Visit to the South Seas, in the U.S. Ship* Vincennes, *during the Years 1829 and 1830* (Haven, N.Y., 1831 [1829]), 143–146.

92. Gorham Gilman, Lahaina in Early Days, *Thrum's Hawaiian Almanac and Annual for 1907,* 171. The writings of businessman Gilman seem breezy and candid in comparison to the ponderous style of some of the missionaries. His work is considered highly credible, as it seems evident that he not only socialized successfully with the missionaries but also was at the center of the not-quite-Christian court life enacted at Moku'ula and at the *ali'i* compound at nearby Pākalā.

93. Community Planning, Inc., Proposal for the Historical Restoration and Preservation of Lahaina, Island of Maui, State of Hawaii (Board of Supervisors, 1961), 36.

94. Foreign Testimony 84.16, 3 June 1854, Hawaii State Archives. See note 150.

95. Valerio Valeri, The Transformation of a Transformation: A Structural Essay on an Aspect of Hawaiian History (1809–1819), Social Analysis 10(1982), 11.

96. Valeri, Transformation, 30.

97. Jane Silverman, *Kaahumanu: Molder of Change* (Friends of the Judiciary History Center of Hawaii, Honolulu, 1987), 101–118.

98. Bingham, *Residence,* 426.

99. Kamakau, *Ruling Chiefs,* 285. Roger Rose, *Reconciling the Past: Two Basketry Ka'ai and the Legendary Liloa and Lonikamakahiki* (Bishop Museum Press, Honolulu, 1992).

100. Richards and Stewart, Letter to *Missionary Herald,* 41.

Chapter 4

101. Marjorie Sinclair, *Nāhi'ena'ena: Sacred Daughter of Hawai'i* (University Press of Hawaii, Honolulu, 1976). In reconstructing the lifestyle at the residence of Kauikeaouli on Moku'ula, I have benefitted from the psychological profiles of several of the leading figures of the time provided by contemporary writers such as Sinclair and Lilikalā Kame'eleihiwa, *Native Land and Foreign Desires* (Bishop Museum Press, Honolulu, 1992). The conflict between traditional and Western routes to power and authority among the *ali'i* of Hawai'i in the early nineteenth century is an important theme in this report. The overarching theories of Kame'eleihiwa and other scholars such as Marshall Sahlins, *Historical Ethnology,* Vol. 1 of *Anahulu: The Anthropology of History in the Kingdom of Hawaii,* edited by Patrick V. Kirch and Marshall Sahlins (University of Chicago Press, Chicago, 1992), have greatly influenced the conceptual and organizational design of this study.

102. Kamakau, *Ruling Chiefs,* 278.

103. Kamakau, *Ruling Chiefs,* 283, 292.

104. See, e.g., Sahlins, *Historical Ethnology.*

105. See Speakman, *Mowee,* 92.

106. On events associated with the rebellion, see Kamakau, *Ruling Chiefs,* 336–351.

107. *Hulumanuweka* means "birds with foul feathers"; see Kamakau, *Ruling Chiefs,* 279. The group represented the living body of supporters of the king, in an allusion to the feather capes (*'ahu'ula*)

and helmets *(mahiole)* of the *ali'i* (see Sahlins, *Historical Ethnology,* 123), in this case used with derision.

108. The site of Kahale'uluhe is near the intersection of modern Beretania and Alapa'i Streets in Honolulu.

109. Kame'eleihiwa, *Native Land,* 113.

110. Sinclair, *Nāhi'ena'ena,* 143.

111. Stephen Reynolds, cited in Sahlins, *Historical Ethnology,* 125.

112. Marshall Sahlins, *Islands of History* (University of Chicago Press, Chicago, 1987), 19.

113. As Rubellite Kawena Johnson has stated, such broader understandings are "strictly pertinent to the salvation of the Hawaiian ego and identity"; Rubellite Kawena Johnson, Hawaiian Literature in English Syllabus (Ms. on file, Department of Indo-Pacific Languages, University of Hawai'i, Mānoa, 1989), 60.

114. *Sandwich Islands Gazette,* 7 January 1837.

115. Kamakau, *Ruling Chiefs,* 342.

116. *Sandwich Islands Gazette,* 21 January 1837.

117. Kamakau, *Tales and Traditions,* 49.

118. Valerio Valeri, *Kingship and Sacrifice* (University of Chicago Press, Chicago, 1985), 22.

119. See Ralph Linton, Nativistic Movements, *American Anthropologist* 45(1943):230–239.

120. Kamakau, *Ruling Chiefs,* 341.

121. Kame'eleihiwa, *Native Land,* 114–115.

122. Andelusia Lee Conde, Journal entry, 11 December 1837, Hawaiian Missionary Children's Society, Honolulu.

123. Mary Ives, Journal entry, 14 December 1837, Hawaiian Missionary Children's Society, Honolulu.

124. Kamakau, *Ruling Chiefs,* 351–352.

125. *Missionary Herald,* 1 July 1833, 30(8):283, 287.

126. W. D. Alexander, Overthrow of the Ancient Tabu System in the Hawaiian Islands, *Twenty-fifth Annual Report of the Hawaiian Historical Society for the Year 1916* (Hawaiian Historical Society, Honolulu, 1917), 45.

127. Sahlins, *Historical Ethnology,* 126.

128. Other nativistic movements in Hawai'i were syncretic in their nature, combining elements of the old order with Christianity. One prominent example was a 1830s cult centered at Puna, Hawai'i, that worshiped a trinity of Jehovah, Jesus, and a dead prophetess named Hapu. See J. J. Jarves, *History of the Hawaiian or Sandwich Islands* (J. Monroe, Boston, 1843), 262.

129. Kamakau, *People of Old,* 83.

130. Sahlins, *Historical Ethnology,* 127–129.

131. Charles Wilkes, *Narrative of the United States Exploring Expedition during the Years 1838–1842,* Vol. 4 (Lea and Blanchard, Philadelphia, 1845), 3–4.

132. See Kame'eleihiwa, *Native Land,* 75, 125. Kamakau, *Ruling Chiefs,* 300.

133. Laura Fish Judd, quoted in Sahlins, *Historical Ethnology,* 110.

134. Kuykendall, *Hawaiian Kingdom,* 153–169.

135. Kamakau, *Ruling Chiefs,* 342. Descended from Alapaʻinui, Julia Alapaʻi married Keoni Ana on 5 August 1829; see Stephen Reynolds, *Journal of Stephen Reynolds,* Vol. 1 (1823–1829) (Ku Paʻa, Honolulu and Peabody Museum, Salem, Mass., 1989), 273.

136. Giniʻs husband J. Kaʻeo had property in Puakō just north of Pākalā in Lahaina, most notably the site of the modern Burger King on Front Street. A parking lot now exists just behind this lot where a fishpond had once been.

137. Alfons Korn, *News from Molokai: Letters between Peter Kaeo and Queen Emma, 1873–1876* (University of Hawaii Press, Honolulu, 1976), 16.

138. Clarice Taylor, Tales about Hawaii, *Honolulu Star-Bulletin,* 10, 11 March 1958:32.4.

139. Henriques Genealogy, 17 Microfilm, 232.2:284, Bishop Museum Archives, Honolulu.

140. Wilkes, *Narrative,* 4–7.

141. Taylor, Tales about Hawaii, 32.4.

142. Steen Bille, quoted in Gerrit P. Judd IV, *Dr. Judd: Hawaii's Friend* (University of Hawaii Press, Honolulu, 1960), 81.

143. Laura Fish Judd, *Honolulu: Sketches of Life in the Hawaiian Islands from 1828–1861* (Lakeside Press, Chicago, 1966), 208.

144. Gilman, Lahaina in Early Days, 173–174.

145. George Simpson, *Overland Journey Round the World during the Years 1841 and 1842* (Ye Galleon Press, 1988 [1841–42]), 64–65. Timothy Haʻalilio subsequently visited Europe with Dr. Judd seeking recognition of the Hawaiian kingdom. He died in France.

146. Gilman, Lahaina in Early Days, 174–175.

147. Kamehameha III to John Halstead, Letter, 22 September 1841, Hawaii State Archives.

148. M. D. Monsarrat, Map of Mokuʻula (n.d.), and W. D. Alexander, Crown Survey Map of Mokuʻula (1855), Bureau of Conveyances, Honolulu; S. E. Bishop, Town of Lahaina, Hawaii Government Survey Map (1884), Reg. Map 1262, Hamilton Library, University of Hawaii, Honolulu.

149. Boundary Commission Award of July 1879. Hawaii State Archives, Honolulu.

150. The legal documents of the Great Mahele of 1848–55, especially the Native and Foreign Registers and Testimonies, provide not only a precise record of land tenure in the Mokuhinia area but also rich insight into family structure, relationships of commoners to chiefs, subsistence and habitation patterns, and political alliances over a broad period of time in the nineteenth century. Primary materials relating to the registration of a claim (Native and Foreign Registry [NR, FR]) and witnessed testimony to the nature of the land claim (Native and Foreign Testimony [NT, FT]) provide a wealth of information on ancient place names, boundaries, landscape features, preexisting political arrangements, and land tenure. The registers and testimony records are potentially misleading, however. Written by the claimants themselves or their agents, these documents often state place names and refer to neighbors in a manner that is not necessarily corroborated by those neighbors. Neighbors did not necessarily know which individual of the adjacent lands would actually claim their land. As a result, multiple names and different references appear. Cross-referencing between the different records often can reconcile these difficulties.

In most cases, Land Commission Awards provide a survey and plan of individual land parcels which are useful in contributing to an understanding of the cultural geography in 1848.

Subsequent documents such as Grants and Boundary Commission Awards have been found to contain information relating not only to land tenure change but to traditional patterns as well.

151. Edith Kawelohea McKinzie, *Hawaiian Genealogies,* Vol. 2 (Brigham Young University, Laie, Hawai'i, 1983), 57.

152. Gilman, Lahaina in Early Days, 170.

153. Fornander, *Polynesian Race,* 2:204.

154. Kamakau, *Ruling Chiefs,* 302.

155. Amy C. Richardson, Genealogy of William Shaw Richardson, 1972, Ms. in collection of P. C. Klieger.

156. Keoni Ana to James Kānehoa, Letter, 23 September 1848. Hawaii State Archives.

157. The older land tenure and boundary system of the village of Kou, Nu'uanu, O'ahu, also began to dissolve when Kamehameha I set up his court here in 1809. The beginning of the city of Honolulu radiated from this royal nucleus; see Klieger in Lebo, Culture Change in Early Honolulu, 7–32.

158. *Indices of Awards Made by the Board of Land Commissioners to Quiet Land Titles in the Hawaiian Islands* (Territory of Hawaii, 1929), 52.

159. Journal of Miriam Kekāuluohi, 1840, 2, Lunalilo Papers, Hawaii State Archives.

160. Kekāuluohi Journal, 2–7.

161. Kame'eleihiwa, *Native Land,* 129.

162. Gilman, Lahaina in Early Days, 175.

163. Laura Green and Mary Pukui, *The Legend of Kawelo and Other Hawaiian Folk Tales* (Territory of Hawaii, Honolulu, 1936), 122–123.

164. Chester S. Lyman, *Around the Horn to the Sandwich Islands and California, 1845–1850* (Yale University Press, New Haven, Conn., 1924), 178.

165. Kuykendall, *Hawaiian Kingdom,* 304–307.

166. Victoria Kamāmalu, daughter of *kuhina nui* Kīna'u, resumed the hereditary nature of the position between 1846 and 1866, although the title was now hollow.

167. G. Judd, *Hawaii's Friend,* 81. L. F. Judd, *Honolulu,* 206.

168. Kuykendall, *Hawaiian Kingdom,* 240.

169. *The Polynesian,* 26 December 1846, 3:32.

170. Malo, *Hawaiian Antiquities,* 191; Ii, *Fragments,* 64–65.

Chapter 5

171. Kamakau, *Ruling Chiefs,* 416–430.

172. F. Gerstaecker, *Narrative of a Journey Around the World* (New York, 1853).

173. Kame'eleihiwa, *Native Land,* 292.

174. Death of Prince Albert Kūkailimoku Kānuiakea, *Hawaiian Gazette,* 11 March 1903. Barbara Bennet Peterson, *Notable Women of Hawaii* (University of Hawaii Press, Honolulu, 1984), 185. Gwen Allen, Queen Kalama, *Honolulu Star-Bulletin,* 20 July 1957:4.

175. A Thurston to G. Gilman, Interior Department letter, 18 May 1852, Hawaii State Archives.

176. Gilman, Lahaina in Early Days, 171.

177. Gorham Gilman to William Webster, Interior Department letter, 19 August 1857, Hawaii State Archives.

178. Bureau of Conveyances, Liber 12:15–16. Office of Tax Management, Honolulu.

179. Charles Warren Stoddard, *The Island of Tranquil Delights* (Herbert B. Turner, Boston, 1905), 285–291. The writings of Stoddard, Alfons Korn, and Isabella Bird paint a Victorian picture of Lahaina in the 1850s to 1870s. Although fictionalized, Stoddard's work seems consistent with the basic facts about Lahaina, as can be seen in comparison with more realistic accounts.

180. George Washington Bates, *Sandwich Island Notes (by a Haole)* (Harper and Brothers, New York, 1854).

181. L. F. Judd, Composition 1., 1850s. Ms. in L. J. Dickson File, Hawaiian Missionary Children's Society.

182. Cracroft quoted in A. Korn, *The Victorian Visitors* (University of Hawaii Press, Honolulu, 1958), 45–46.

183. Rufus Anderson, *The Hawaiian Islands: Their Progress and Conditions under Missionary Labour* (Gould and Lincoln, Boston, 1864).

184. Inventory of the Estate of Hoapili-wahine, 64, Lunalilo Papers, 1842, Hawaii State Archives.

185. Kristin Zambucka, *The High Chiefess Ruth Keelikolani* (Mana, Honolulu, 1977), 57.

186. Richardson, Genealogy of William Shaw Richardson.

187. Inventory of Hoapili-wahine, Lunalilo Papers, 64.

188. This may be Nueku Nāmauʻu, a relative of Oʻahu governor Kekūanaoʻa and an associate of Kauikeaouli; see Kameʻeleihiwa, *Native Land,* 265.

189. Probate 35, 2nd Circuit Court, 1859, Lahaina; Probate 301 1st Circuit Court, Supreme Court, Honolulu 1859, Court Records, Honolulu.

190. Kameʻeleihiwa, *Native Land,* 276.

191. Boundary Commission Award, July 1879, Hawaii State Archives. Translated by Nancy King Holt.

192. Auwae was probably a *hānai* child of Hoapili. During a meeting of chiefs in February 1842, he testified before Kekāuluohi that he never received any land from Hoapili because a foreigner had performed all his duties for Hoapili and received property in exchange; see Kekāuluohi Journal, 17, Lunalilo Papers.

193. Sahlins (*Historical Ethnology*) notes this attitude among *aliʻi* elsewhere in Hawaiʻi.

194. George Kanahele, *Pauahi* (Kamehameha Schools Press, Honolulu, 1986). A sore point among many contemporary Native Hawaiians, Kamehameha I left many descendants, most of whom were declared illegitimate under Western concepts of propriety. Perhaps the most upset of all was Albert, child of Kamehameha III and Gini Lahilahi, who may otherwise have been his father's successor.

195. Kaʻae quoted in I. Ashdown, *The Story of Lahaina* (Taylor, Dallas, 1947).

196. Bureau of Conveyances, Liber 115:169, Office of Tax Management, Honolulu.

197. Rose, *Reconciling the Past,* 28.

198. Turner, Tombs of *Ali'i*.

199. Jesse Condé and Gerald Best, *Sugar Trains* (Glenwood, Felton, Calif., 1973), 252.

200. Community Planning Inc., Proposal for Historical Restoration, 40.

201. Ashdown, miscellaneous letters and notes, Ms. on file, Anthropology Department, Bishop Museum, Honolulu.

202. Turner, Tombs of *Ali'i*.

203. Written in 1862 by P. H. Kekuaiwa, cited in *Hula o Nā Keiki* (Kā'anapali Beach Hotel, Maui, 1993). Mānoanoa is the name of a chiefess who once lived at Moku'ula.

Appendix

204. Reported in Klieger, ed., Moku'ula: History and Archaeological Excavations.

205. Charlene Cerny and Suzanne Seriff, eds., *Recycled: Re-seen* (Harry Abrams and the Museum of New Mexico, 1996).

206. In 1995, the Maui County Burial Council authorized public dissemination of information that human remains were recovered. Bishop Museum reported the details of this recovery to the State of Hawaii, Department of Land and Natural Resources.

Index

(Boldface indicates illustration.)

ahupua'a, 5, 69, 78
  defined by watersheds, 15, 91
  in Kalua'ehu, 62–63, 65–66
'Aikanaka, 16, 71
aikāne, 42, 44, 47, 50, 53–54
'ainoa, 25, 39, 52
Alapa'i, Julia, 53–54, 58, 74
Alapa'inui, 18–19, 68
Albert Kūnuiākea Kūkā'ilimoku, Prince, 53, 81
Alexander, William P., 61, 71, 89
Alexander Liholiho, King Kamehameha IV, 81–82
American Board of Commissions for Foreign Missions, 25
Anderson, Rufus, 86–87
Arago, Jacques, 28
Ashdown, Inez, 31, 93

Baldwin Packers, 97
Bates, George Washington, 84
Bingham, Hiram, 30, 37–38
Bishop, Bernice Pauahi, 64, 93–94
Bishop, Charles Reed, 94
Bishop, S. E., 36, 61–63, 89, 92
Blonde, H.M.S., 33
Bloxam, Richard, 32
Boki, 33–34, 38, 41, 44, 82
Boundary Commission, testimony, 89–92
Brayton, George, 83
"Brick house," in Lahaina, 26, 64

Cleopatra's Barge, 27
Conde, Andelusia Lee, 48–49
Constitution of 1840, 53
Cook, Capt. James, 37
Cracroft, Sophia, 84–86
creation myth (Kumulipo), 7, 44
Crown Land, 58, 60, 62–63, 65–66, 70, 72, 87, 89–90, 96

De Freycinet, Louis, 26, 27
Delphi, python, 46
Duperrey map of Lahaina, 32
dyarchy of rule, 36–37, 53

'e'epa, 9, 15
electromagnetic resistivity, 101
Ellis, William, 32–33
Emma, Queen, 81–82, 84–85

fort, Lahaina, 31–32, 54

George IV, King of Great Britain and Ireland, 33
Gilman, Gorham, 35–36, 56–58, 64, 70, 72, 82, 84
Gold Rush, California, 73, 79
"Great Awakening," 50–53
Green, Laura, 72

Ha'alilo, Timothy, **47**, 56–57, 72
Hālawa, O'ahu, 13
hale o Papa, 11, 14
Hale Piula, 2, 5, 40, 45, 53, 56, **60, 62,** 70, 73, 76–77, 105
  description, 54, 58–59, 84
hale puaniu, 14, 22
Halehuki, 45
Halekamani, 29–32, 34–35, **36,** 40, 44–45, **62,** 66, 70, 81
  tomb remodeled as residence, 82–84
Hana, chiefs, 8
Harris, Charles Coffin, 81
heiau, 2, 11, 13, 15–16, 22, 26, 29–30, 38, 52
Hoapili, Ulumaheihei, 17, 22, 24, 27–29, 32, 34–35, 39, 42, 44, 46, **47,** 51–53, 62, 65–67, 70–72, 82, 87, 89–90, 94, 96
Honolulu, 3, 22, 34, 41–43, 50, 66, 72–77, 81
  prophecy on capital move, 72–74, 80, 82, 94, 108
Ho'ohōkūikalani, 8
Hulumanu, 42, 47, 56, 74, 80

'Ī'ī, John Papa, 11, 22, 77
'Iolani Palace, 74, 80–81
Ives, Mary, 49

Judd, Gerrit, 75
Judd, Laura Fish, 56, 75, 84

Ka'ae, Alice, 88–89, 93
Ka'ahumanu, Queen, 25, 28, 32, 34, 36–39, 49, 51–53, 55, 82, 108
  death and burial, 42
  destroys ancient burial sites, 38, 41
kā'ai, 29, 38
Ka'eo, Gini Lahilahi Young, 47, 53, 65
Kahale'uluhe Palace, 41, 43
Kaheiheimālia, Queen, 25, 34, 51–54, 65, 82, 87–88
Kahekili I, 8, 16

Kahekili II, King, 16–17, 19–20, 24, 34, 44, 49, 54, 72
Kahekilike'eaumoku, 23, 26, 34, 67
kahili, 30, **40**, 48–49, 64
Kaikio'ewa, 24, 26–27, 43
Kaiko'okalani, 35, 44
Kailikauohu, 34–35, 44
Kalā'aiheana; see Kihawahine
kālai'āina, 61, 71
Kalaipaihala, 62–63, 65–67
Kalākaua, King, 15–16, 71, 94
Kalama, Queen, 46, 50, 53, 56, 58, **76**, 80–81, 89–91
  property in Lahaina, 62, 68
  tried by Church, 54–56
Kalama'ula, Moloka'i, 9
Kalanikauiōkikilokalaniakua, 16–19, 21, 23
Kalanikūpule, 16, 20–21, 235
Kalanimoku, 26–28, 31, 33–34, 36, 43–44
Kalani'ōpu'u, 18, 21, 37–38, 54
Kalola Pupuka, 16–21, 23–24, 37
Kalua o Kiha, 2, 5, 12, 31–33, 51, 58, 61, **62**, 64, 70, 74
  konohiki of fishponds, 92
Kalua'ehu, 5, 15, 31, 40, 58, 61, 64–66, 69–70, 74, 87, 92, 109
Kamakau, Samuel, 10, 12–14, 18, 45–46, 49, 79
Kamāmalu, Princess Victoria, 65, 74
Kamāmalu, Queen, 28, 33–34, 53, 81
Kamehameha I, King, 2, 10, 16–17, 19, 22–25, 32, 34, 36–37, 44, 54, 58, 64–65, 67–68, 71–72, 82, 91, 93–94, 98–99, 108
Kamehameha II, King; see Liholiho
Kamehameha III, King; see Kauikeaouli
Kamehameha IV, King; see Alexander Liholiho
Kamehameha V, King; see Lota Kapuāiwa
Kamehamehanui, 16–18, 30, 93
Kana'ina, Charles, 46, 64
Kānehoa, James Young, 33, 68, 76
Kānekua'ana, 13–14
Kaomi, 42–44, 48, 54
Ka'opulupulu, 72–73
kapu moe, 17–18
kapu system, 1–2, 9–10, 15, 25–26, 46
  haole system of protocol, 75
  physical demarcation, 77–78
Kaua'ula Stream, 6, 16, 18, 66–67, 99
  winds, 84
Kauikeaouli (King Kamehameha III), 1–3, 5, 7–8, 26–29, **34**, 35–40, **41**, 43–48, 52–58, 61–62, 64–75, **76**, 77, 82, 87, 90–91, 98–99, 105–109
  birth, 23

  cohabitation with Nāhi'ena'ena, 43–44
  death and burial, 79, **80**, 81
  drinking, 49–50
  early childhood, 24
  emancipation from Ka'ahumanu, 42–43
  end of *kapu,* 25
Kaumuali'i, King, 23, 28, 82
  death and burial, 32–33, 44, 83
Keaweawe'ulaokalani I and II, 53, 54, 82
Ke'elikōlani, Princess Ruth, 87–89
Kekau'ōnohi, 34, 36, 47, 66, 82
Kekaulike, 16–17, 44, 71
Kekāuluohi, Premier Auhea Miriam, 37–38, 46, 51–52, 70, 82, 87–88
  attacked by *mo'o,* 50
  property description, 64, 71–72, 74
Kekūāiwa Kamehameha, 23
Kekūanaō'a, 33, 43, 64–65, 74, 81, 87
Keku'iapoiwa Liliha, 16, 18–19, 21, 23
Kelea, 8–9, 16
Keoni Ana, Premier, 47, 53–54, 56–57, 64–65, 68, **74**, 76, 79–81
Keōpūolani, Queen, 18–25, 27, 32, 34–38, 40, 44–45, 52, 64, 71–72
  bestowal of name, 21
  death and burial 28, **29**, 30–31, 81, 83, 85–86, 94
Kihaapi'ilani, 8, 12, 16
Kihawahine Mokuhinia Kalama'ula Kalā'aiheana, 2, 9, 10, **11**, 12–18, 22–23, 32, 37, 39, 40, 45–47, 50–51, 66, 70, 87, 89, 92
Kiliwehi, 35, 44
Kīna'u, Premier, 37, 39, 43, 49, 50, 52, 55, 65, 81
"King's Rebellion," 42–43
Kīwala'ō (father of Keōpūolani), 16, 18–19, 37–38
Kīwala'ō (son of Kamehameha III), 53
Kū, 8, 37
Kūkā'ilimoku, 21
Kukuloia, Honolulu, 22, 66
Kukuloia, Lahaina, 47, **62**, 66–67, 72, 89
Kumulipo, 44

La'anui, Gideon, 23
Lahaina, 1–2, 3, **4**, 5, **6**, 9, 12, **15**, 16–19, 22–23, 26–28, 31, 33–35, 38–39, 45, 49, 52–54, **59**, 61, **62–63**, 66, 68–69, **70**, 73, 76, 78, 81–85, **86**, 87, **89**, 90, **92**, 94, **95–98**, 101, **102**, 105
  devastation, 18–20
  restoration, 22
Lailai, 11

Leleiōhoku, 43
Liholiho (King Kamehameha II), 22, 25–26, 28, 32, 44, 64, 71, 80–81
Liliha, Premier, 33–35, 38, 41–42, 49–50, 52, 57, 65, 71–72, 65, 82
Lili'uokalani, Queen, 15–16, 82
longue durée, 37
Lono, path of, 37
Lonoapi'ilani, 9, 16
Lota Kapuāiwa (King Kamehameha V), 62, 66, 68, 71–72, 87–90, 98
Luakaha, O'ahu, 73–74, **75**
Lu'aunuialepokapo, 73
Ludwig II, King of Bavaria, 77
Lunalilo, King William Charles, 62, 64–66, 70, 72, 92
Lyman, Chester, 73

Macrae, James, 31–32
Mahele, Great, 36, 58–59, 61–66, 69–70, 72, 79–80, 90, 92
Makahiki, 9, 10, 15, 23, 43
Malo, David, 47, 77
  property, 62–63, 65
Malu'ulu o Lele County Park 3–4, 96–97
Manu, Moses, 12
material culture, *mana,* 107, 110
Mauna 'Ala, Nu'uanu, O'ahu (Royal Mausoleum), 42, 81, 93–94
Menzies, Archibald, 20
missionaries, 2, 25, 27, 34, 36, 44–45, 48–50, 52–53, 56–57, 77, 80
moku, meanings, 1
Mokuhinia, Loko o, 1–3, 5–7, 9, 12–13, 15–16, 23, 31, 39, 40, 45–47, 50–52, 58–61, **62**, 63–66, 68, 70, 81, 84, 86–87, 89–94, 96–99, 101, 103–106, 109, 110
Moku'ula
  archaeological discoveries at, 98–99, 101–110
  chant, 99
  commutation by Lunalilo, 70, 92
  covering over, 96, 98
  creation of island, 105–106
  description, 48–49, 55–57, 84
  first resident, 34
  holding ponds, 59
  last visit by King Kamehameha III, 76
  meanings, 1–2
  partition, 89–93
  place of *kapu,* location, 3–4
  tomb, **59, 60, 62,** 77–78, 81–83, 85, 93, **94**
Monsarrat, M. D., 58, 60–61, 70, 89

mo'o, 2, 5, 7–9, 12, **13,** 42, 45, 47, 51–52, 70, 93
  and disease, 23, 46, 79–80
  sightings, 23, 38, 50–52
Mo'oinaea, ancestral *mo'o,* 8, 16

Na'ea, Fanny Young, 47, 62, 65–66, 84, **85**
Nāhi'ena'ena, Princess, 12, 23, 26–29, 33–36, 39, **40,** 41–43, 48, 55, 64, 66, 70–71, 82–83, 90–91, 106
  death and burial 44–46, 49
Nalehu, 68, 88–90
Napaepae, 59, 68, 90–91
Nīhoa, Honolulu, 32
Nu'uanu Pali, battle of, 21

Pākākā, 22, 26, 32–33, 66, 77–78
Pākalā, 23, 31, **62,** 64–66
Pākī, Abner, 38, 43, 47
  property in Lahaina, 62, 64–66
Papa, 7–8, 15, 21
"Paulet Affair," 72, 75
Pearl Harbor, 'Ewa, O'ahu, 13–14, 43–44
peleleu, 22, 68
Pi'ikea, 9, 16
Pi'ilani, 9–10, 15–16, 19, 45
  lineage, 9, 15–18, 21
Pikanele, 62, 65–66
piko, 2, 37, 40, 46
pi'o marriage, 8, 15, 17, 21, 43, 44, 46, 54, 64
Pioneer Mill Co., 94, 96
Pohukaina, Honolulu, O'ahu, 34, 42, 74, 77
pollen analysis, 103–105
Pukui, Mary Kawena, 72
Punahou wall, 41
punalua, 42–43, 54, 65, 71, 73, 88
punawai, at Moku'ula, 59, 90
pu'uhonua, 13
Pu'uloa, 'Ewa, O'ahu, 43–44

radiocarbon dating, Mokuhinia, 103–104
revitalization, Hawaiian religion, 38, 49–50
Richards, William, 27, 30, 43, 50, 53, 72
Rooke, T. C. B., 43, 80

Sahlins, Marshall, 44, 50
sandalwood, 41
Sawkins, James, 58–59
sediment cores, 101, 103–105
Shaw family, 60, 62, 68, 87–90, 93–94, 97, **98**
Simpson, George, 56–57
Sinclair, Marjorie, 39
Sociopolitical system, 5, 64, 79
  archaeological interpreation, 108–109

political geometry, 69, 70, 74, 77–78, 87
Speakman, Cummins, 33
Stewart, C. S., 27–31, 35–36
Stoddard, Charles, 83–84

taro (*kalo*), 6, 8, 19, 22, 26, 28, 56, 58, 66–67,
    103, 105
Thrum, Thomas, 31
Turner, Charlotte, 94

'ula, meaning, 1–2
'Ulu lineage, 8
Ulumaheiheihoapili; *see* Hoapili
'Umialīloa, 9, 16
unification, wars of, 18–21
'Uo Beach, 6, **62**, 64
Uyehara, Mitsuo, 32

Vancouver, Capt. George, 19–20

Wahine Pi'o, (Kahakuha'akoi), 34, 44–45, 106
Wahine Pi'o, (Keōpūolani), 21
Waikīkī, 22
Wailehua Heiau, 16, 29–30
Wailuku chiefs, 8–9, 16
Waine'e *ahupua'a,* 5, 52, **62–63,** 65–71, 87
    boundary with Waiokama, 89–93, 99
Waine'e Church, 39, 47, 50, 52, **59, 62,** 84, **86,**
    87, 90, 93–94, 96–97, 110
Waiokama, 5, 60, **62,** 66, 68–69, 87–94, 97
Waiola Church, 5
Wākea, 7–8, 15, 21
whaling, 73, 79
Wilkes, Charles, 54–55
Wyllie, Robert C., 75

Young, John Sr., 47, 57, 85
    family, 64–66